Terryann Scott
NO MORE BARRIERS

Roads to Success:
No More Barriers
Volume 2 of *"The 'No More' Series"*

Scripture quotations are from the King James Version of the Holy Bible (KJV).

© 2014 Terryann Scott

All rights reserved. No part of this book may be reproduced or transmitted in any form or by any means, electronically or mechanically, without permission in writing from the author.
Please note that certain nouns have not been capitalized, such as satan and other related counterparts. This is intentional as homage is not credited to such.

eBook Edition:
ISBN: 978-976-95696-3-8
ASIN: B00NC3AWY6

Print Edition
ISBN: 978-976-95696-2-1

All correspondence should be addressed to:
info.scottspublishing@gmail.com

Cover Design:
Danever Scott

BOOKS BY THIS AUTHOR

Becoming a Better You: Heal Your Soul; Heal Your Life
Keys to the Kingdom: Unlocking the Mystery of Prayer
The Revelation of the Dragon: No More Walls
Roads to Success: No More Barriers
Overcoming Obstacles: Hope Devotional
Surviving Challenging Times: Faith Devotional
Finding God: Love Devotional
Hidden Truths: Daily Devotional
Sixty-One Thoughts That Can Change Your Life:
Wisdom Nuggets

----

*This book is dedicated to the
Church -- to every Believer in Christ.
Also, to the Godhead;
Father, Son, and Holy Spirit.*

"Blessed are the poor in spirit, for theirs is the Kingdom of heaven."
(Matthew 5:3)

CONTENTS

Acknowledgments   11

Introduction   13
1. The Heart Path   17
2. The Road of Relationship   31
3. Purity Road   41
4. The Road of Freedom   65
5. Determination Drive   79
6. Confidence Avenue   87
7. The Choice Path   105
8. Four Principles For Success   123

About the Author   151
Let's Connect   155
Books by Terryann Scott   157

ACKNOWLEDGMENTS

I would like to thank everyone involved throughout this publication process.

A special thank you goes out to my teacher and friend, the Holy Spirit. This book would not have been possible without Him.

Lord, I thank you for all the lessons you've taught me through the precious gift of life, including the hurdles and challenges that come with it. I am grateful. May this book serve as a tool to impact, influence, and bring change to the lives of those who seek You.

A special thank you goes to my husband, Danever Scott, for the cover design of this book. Thank you also for the time you took to listen and for the suggestions regarding the material you shared.

Thanks to my mother, Aneita Brown, for lending me her ears and sharing her thoughts on this book.

I also thank you, my readers, for taking the time to genuinely read and reflect on the material in this book. Please read slowly and meditate on the scriptures shared.

May God bless you all, and may you experience His transforming power in your life.

INTRODUCTION

There's a heartfelt concern I want to share about the church as a whole. It seems like there's a lack of knowledge, productivity, and prosperity all around us, and sometimes it feels like we're living in darkness without even realizing it. But the beautiful promise in 3 John 1:2 reminds us of God's true desire for us. The verse says, *"Beloved, I wish above all things* (especially highlighting the word ALL), *That thou may prosper and be in health, even as thy soul prospereth."* God's wish for us goes beyond spiritual growth—He wants us to succeed and be healthy in every aspect of our lives. Isn't that an inspiring thought to ponder?

It is clear that there is a lack of knowledge, and the unfortunate reality is that God cannot fulfill His role until the church starts to do her part correctly.

> *"Lest Satan should get an advantage of us: for we are not ignorant of his devices"* (2 Corinthians 2:11).

I speak from my personal experience and the lessons learned. Although I have been a Christian for many years and active in the church, I was initially unaware of much of God's Word and spiritual truths. I genuinely loved God and believed I had given Him my whole heart, thinking I was doing my best for Him, though I knew I could improve. My true transformation began during a profound search for truth, which I described in *"The Revelation of the Dragon: No More Walls Vol. 1."* It was during this search that I realized I was not yet truly transformed into His likeness. As I submitted my ways to Him, my eyes were gradually opened to His truths and the reality around me.

God has so much for us. He wants to bless His people more than we could ever imagine, but He has given us free will, so the decision is ours. If we desire what God has for us, we must abide by HIS laws. God laid out the conditions for us, and the choice is ours to accept or reject them.

> *"But as it is written, Eye hath not seen, nor ear heard, neither have entered into the heart of man,*

INTRODUCTION

the things which God hath prepared for them that love Him" (1 Corinthians 2:9).

"I call heaven and earth to record this day against you, that I have set before you life and death, blessing and cursing: therefore, choose life, that both thou and thy seed may live" (Deuteronomy 30:19):

"If ye be willing and obedient, ye shall eat the good of the land" (Isaiah 1:19):

To truly experience God's fullness, start by being honest with yourself. To receive His blessings, follow His commandments. If you desire freedom and success, continue reading.

I am excited to share seven processes and four principles that everyone can follow to become successful and experience God's blessings and power in their lives. I refer to these processes as roads and paths because they are indeed spiritual pathways we must travel daily for guaranteed success. I believe your life will change dramatically once you apply the insights from this book. Transformation will occur as your perspectives shift and you stay receptive to Him. As your flaws become evident, you'll gain a deeper awareness of God's presence and His glory. Chains will be broken, and strongholds will be demolished through God's power.

May His presence and blessings be with you as you start your journey toward a new, transformed life in Him – the life God wants you to live.

1
THE HEART PATH

"Keep thy heart with all diligence; for out of it are the issues of life" (Proverbs 4:23).

Before I start, I think it's important to first consider some conditions of the heart to establish a solid foundation, helping everything to be understood clearly. According to the Full Life Study Bible, the definition of heart given – and I'll paraphrase – is "The center and director of human activity, containing the totality of one's intellect, emotions, and volition." Regarding intellect, people consider things in their hearts (Deuteronomy 8:5), meditate in their hearts (Psalm 19:14), commune with themselves (Psalm 77:6) or with God (1

Samuel 1:12-13) in their hearts, hide God's Word in their hearts (Psalm 119:11), keep things in their hearts (Proverbs 4:21), imagine things in their hearts (Psalm 140:2), reason in their hearts (Mark 2:8), doubt in their hearts (Mark 11:23), ponder in their hearts (Luke 2:19), believe in their hearts (Romans 10:9), and sing in their hearts (Ephesians 5:19). All of these actions of the heart are primarily mental.

Regarding the emotions, the Scriptures speak of the glad heart (Exodus 4:14), the loving heart (Deuteronomy 6:5), the fearful heart (Joshua 5:1), the courageous heart (Psalm 27:14), the repentant heart (Psalm 51:17), the heavy heart (Proverbs 12:25), the angry heart (Proverbs 19:3), the pained heart (Jeremiah 4:19), the grieving heart (Lamentations 2:18), the humble heart (Matthew 11:29), and the troubled heart (John 14:1). All of these actions of the heart are primarily emotional in character.

Finally, in relation to the human will, we have read in the Scriptures about the hardened heart that refuses to do what God commands (Exodus 4:21), the heart that is inclined to cling to God (Joshua 24:23) and to obey His testimonies (Psalm 119:36), the heart that intends to do something (2 Chronicles 6:7), the heart that is set to seek the Lord (1 Chronicles 22:19), the heart that decides (2 Chronicles 6:7), the heart that wants to receive from the Lord (Psalm 21:1-2), and the heart that desires to do something (Romans 10:1).

All of these activities take place in the human will – end of quote.

The word 'heart' can sometimes be used interchangeably with 'mind.' Based on the definitions, it's clear I am not referring to the muscular organ that pumps blood, but rather the biblical concept of the heart. Despite this difference, the functions of the heart are similar in both contexts, as it governs the center of life.

The heart is the core of life, serving as the processing center for every thought and action. Our behavior reflects the health of our hearts, which is why Proverbs 4:23 advises us to guard our hearts diligently and persistently. Every challenge we face in life stems from the state of our hearts. This scripture is among the most impactful and one of my personal favorites.

There are many heart conditions in the body of Christ today. So many souls are wounded, and so many people are struggling with hurt. These unhealed wounds will block us from accessing all that God has for us. To receive God's choicest blessings, we must genuinely look within ourselves and allow God to show us where we err, so healing can be administered accordingly. Everything we have endured in life was meant to serve as a foundation to equip us for the mission God has given us and to steer us on the path He wants us to take.

All the challenges you've faced in life—and will continue to face—serve as preparation for your purpose.

These experiences were never meant to hold you back. However, due to our limited understanding, personal desires, and beliefs, we've allowed these difficulties to leave deep wounds and scars that hinder our growth. Many of us are still influenced by our past, which has shaped a new character and belief system that often contradicts God's truths. Consequently, some individuals become stuck or trapped in their own world, unable to move beyond the past from which they have not fully been delivered.

People might think they are free because they no longer feel their past's impact or believe they've moved on since their memories no longer dominate their thoughts. However, this can be misleading if the negative influences of the past still linger in our subconscious. Our behaviors and mindsets are influenced by everything within us, whether we are aware of it or not. If these emotional wounds are left unaddressed, they can prevent us from fully receiving God's promises. It is essential to guard our hearts against the corruption that can threaten us.

"No More Barriers" promises to help the body of Christ address and eradicate these wounds. Before we can think of success God's way, we must first look inward and search our hearts. Continually ask God in prayer to reveal to you the condition of your heart as you study and meditate on His Word.

As I mentioned earlier, there are many kinds of hearts. An obedient heart, a fearful heart, a sad heart, a loving heart, a courageous heart, a rebellious heart, a disobedient heart, a deceitful heart, a faithful heart, and the list goes on. What kind of heart do you have? Allow God to reveal it to you.

> *"The heart is deceitful above all things, and desperately wicked: who can know it?"* (Jeremiah 17:9).

> *"And he said unto them, ye are they which justify yourselves before men; but God knoweth your hearts: for that which is highly esteemed among men is abomination in the sight of God"* (Luke 16:15).

It is one thing to say I have a loving heart, but it is another if God sees differently. There is a fine line between truth and deception, which is why we must allow God to show us our hearts, because He is a discerner of the heart and searches all things. If you say you love God, the truth will be found in your actions and the choices you make, because the proof is not in a confession but in the state of our hearts, which rules our actions. So, if you declare that God comes first in your life, ensure He gets first place by submitting to His standards and ways instead of your own.

Consider these questions. Does everyone and

everything around you come after God? Are your choices influenced by people or other external entities, or are they based on God's Word? Who do you try to please more often, God, man, or yourself? Who impacts your decisions the most? Only you can answer these questions.

Too often, many things take first place in our lives instead of God, and they go unnoticed. It may be easy for you to make a sacrifice to go to work when you are tired or ill, but when it comes to church attendance, little or no sacrifice is made except for dishing out excuses. We hear, preach, teach, and talk about love, yet we remain guilty of ignoring the needy, even of an encouraging word. People often confess without hesitation that God comes first in their lives, yet they remain hearers of the Word rather than doers. People's hearts have turned back from God in many ways, but pride and ignorance have blinded many from seeing the truth. We must rely on God and turn to Him wholeheartedly so that He can show us our current state and help us avoid one of the devil's main ploys – deception.

If we were to consider the lives of exemplary men in the Bible who were anointed and influential, men who had a close relationship with God, we would discover that they all had one thing in common: a heart for God. Jesus is our primary example, but let us look at a few others. King David was called 'a man after God's own heart' according to the book of Acts. Abraham had an obedient heart, and he was called a friend of God (Isaiah 41:8). Moses, the mediator, had a loving heart; his love for God and his relationship with God were outstanding. He saw God, and God proved Himself to him over and over. Their relationship was sealed. Moses not only loved God but also genuinely loved people. Paul and the Apostles, Daniel, and so many more had a fixed heart in God unto death. They were completely sold out, and their hearts played a vital role in their success. In order for God to use and bless you as He desires, it is important for you to have a heart that is fixed in Him; one that will never turn away from God or forget Him, in good times or in bad.

"And thou shalt love the Lord thy God with all thine heart, and with all thy soul, and with all thy might.

And these words, which I command thee this day, shall be in thine heart:

And thou shalt teach them diligently unto thy children, and shalt talk of them when thou sittest in thine house, and when thou walkest by the way, and when thou liest down, and when thou risest up.

And thou shalt bind them for a sign upon thine

hand, and they shall be as frontlets between thine eyes.

And thou shalt write them upon the posts of thy house, and on thy gates.

And it shall be, when the Lord thy God shall have brought thee into the land which he swore unto thy fathers, to Abraham, to Isaac, and to Jacob, to give thee great and goodly cities, which thou buildedst not,

And houses full of all good things, which thou filledst not, and wells digged, which thou diggedst not, vineyards and olive trees, which thou plantedst not; when thou shalt have eaten and be full;

Then beware lest thou forget the Lord, which brought thee forth out of the land of Egypt, from the house of bondage.

Thou shalt fear the Lord thy God, and serve Him, and shalt swear by His name.

Ye shall not go after other gods, of the gods of the people which are round about you;

*(For the Lord thy God is a jealous God among you)
lest the anger of the Lord thy God be kindled
against thee, and destroy thee from off the face of the
earth"* (Deuteronomy 6: 5-15).

This is why everyone experiences a testing period: God aims to try us and reveal what's in our hearts—whether we will consistently obey His Word or succumb to temptation. Although God knows the end from the beginning, our true victory comes through making correct choices. Therefore, He tests us to give us the opportunity to choose for ourselves.

*"All the commandments which I command thee
this day shall ye observe to do, that ye may live, and
multiply, and go in and possess the land which the
Lord swore unto your fathers.*

*And thou shalt remember all the way which the
Lord thy God led thee these forty years in the
wilderness, to humble thee, and to prove thee, to
know what was in thine heart, whether thou
wouldest keep his commandments, or no.*

*And He humbled thee, and suffered thee to hunger,
and fed thee with manna, which thou knewest not,
neither did thy fathers know; that He might make*

thee know that man doth not live by bread only, but by every word that proceedeth out of the mouth of the Lord doth man live.

Thy raiment waxed not old upon thee, neither did thy foot swell, these forty years.

Thou shalt also consider in thine heart, that, as a man chasteneth his son, so the Lord thy God chasteneth thee.

Therefore, thou shalt keep the commandments of the Lord thy God, to walk in His ways, and to fear Him" (Deuteronomy 8: 1-6).

Many of life's struggles stem from issues stored within our hearts. Our problems often arise from the impaired decisions we make. The Bible clearly states that we will be rewarded based on our actions.

"I the LORD search the heart, I try the reins, even to give every man according to his ways, and according to the fruit of his doings" (Jeremiah 17:10).

"For he is the minister of God to thee for good. But if thou do that which is evil, be afraid; for he beareth

not the sword in vain: for he is the minister of God, a revenger to execute wrath upon him that doeth evil" (Romans 13:4).

Our actions are influenced by the condition of our hearts. God's blessing depends on our hearts being correctly aligned with Him; only then will He bless us. We need to pass our spiritual test before we receive a promotion. The current state of the church isn't due to God's unwillingness to bless but rather His protection from harm. Turning away from God or neglecting His Word is a serious matter with grave consequences.

You just read it. God is a jealous God; He will judge us if He blesses us and we prove that we are not mature enough to handle His blessings. It would be like giving a ten-year-old the keys to your car for them to drive. A child cannot handle certain desires; they would only cause harm because they are not ready to manage them. Similarly, we must come of age spiritually in God to be prepared and mature enough to receive certain blessings. Our readiness to receive from God depends on how willing we are to learn and understand His principles. It depends on us— our obedience, faithfulness, hearts, and spiritual maturity in Christ. Please make the time to read 1 Samuel chapters 15 and 16 and meditate on it. A part of it goes like this:

"And it came to pass, when they were come, that he

*looked on Eliab, and said, surely the Lord's
anointed is before him.*

*But the Lord said unto Samuel, look not on his
countenance, or on the height of his stature; because
I have refused him: for the Lord seeth not as man
seeth; for man looketh on the outward appearance,
but the Lord looketh on the heart.*

*Then Jesse called Abinadab, and made him pass
before Samuel. And he said, neither hath the Lord
chosen this.*

*Then Jesse made Shammah pass by. And he said,
neither hath the Lord chosen this.*

*Again, Jesse made seven of his sons pass before
Samuel. And Samuel said unto Jesse, the Lord hath
not chosen these.*

*And Samuel said unto Jesse, are here
all thy children? And he said, there remaineth yet
the youngest, and, behold, he keepeth the sheep. And
Samuel said unto Jesse, send and fetch him: for we
will not sit down till he come hither.*

*And he sent, and brought him in. Now
he was ruddy, and withal of a beautiful countenance,
and goodly to look to. And the Lord said, Arise,
anoint him: for this is he"* (1 Samuel 16:6-12).

Saul lost his kingship due to disobedience, while David was made king because of his obedient heart. What is the condition of your heart today? You might be acknowledged by people, but still go unnoticed by God. Whose approval are you striving for?

Man looks at outward appearance, but God is interested in our hearts. Will you give Him your heart entirely today? Your success depends on it.

Other Scripture References:

1 Samuel 7: 1-17
St. Mark 7: 5-23
1 Kings 15:5
Acts 13:22
St. Mathew 15: 3-20; 23:1-28

TIMELY THOUGHTS

- Your breakthrough lies in your obedience to God.
- Your promotion is tied to the condition of your heart.
- How far you go in life is not determined by God, but by your obedience to Him.

2
THE ROAD OF RELATIONSHIP

"Blessed are they which do hunger and thirst after righteousness: for they shall be filled" (Matthew 5:6).

"But seek ye first the Kingdom of God, and His righteousness; and all these things shall be added unto you" (Matthew 6:33).

A personal relationship with God is the foundation for all other relationships. It is also the core reflection of your inner self. This is something every Believer needs for themselves. We can't depend on someone else's relationship to guide us. If we belong to God, we must recognize His voice and know when He is speaking to us.

> *"My sheep hear my voice, and I know them, and they follow me"* (St. John 10:27):

With so much deception around us, we need to hear from God. Personal closeness is what a relationship with God brings. God is a Spirit, yet you will feel and experience His tangible presence with you everywhere you go. He desires fellowship and communion with us; that is why He made us!

> *"Come now, and let us reason together, saith the LORD: though your sins be as scarlet, they shall be as white as snow; though they be red like crimson, they shall be as wool"* (Isaiah 1:18).

We can develop a relationship with God simply by talking to Him. Think of a natural relationship with someone you can see. A relationship without communication is dead, and if you are the only one talking, it will become frustrating over time. You will only experience fulfillment through fellowship, and this happens when the conversation is mutual and interactive, which in turn allows the relationship to feel alive and meaningful. God is always speaking to us, but we fail to recognize His voice, and He echoes it in many ways.

He speaks to us in our hearts sometimes through a feeling. Have you ever felt the need or urge to go somewhere, and when you did, something worked out in your favor, or if you failed to obey that feeling, the opposite happened, such as a missed opportunity or even tragedy? Well, that was the Holy Spirit speaking to you.

God speaks to us through our minds and thoughts, but sometimes we mistake these thoughts for our own when they are actually from God.

He speaks to us through people by prophecy or through our relationships, and He speaks directly to our spirits audibly in a still, soft voice that sometimes sounds like our own.

God also speaks to us through His Word. He gives comfort, peace, and clear instructions for our situation through His Word. If you want to know the mind of God, get into His Word. If you want to become like Him, study His Word. If you want to know God's will for your life, get into His Word. His Word sanctifies and cleanses. His Word brings change. His Word contains the blueprint for our lives, and as we become conformed to His ways, our minds will be renewed. We are transformed by the power of His Word as we put it into action.

"But we all, with open face beholding as in a glass

the glory of the Lord, are changed into the same image from glory to glory, even as by the Spirit of the Lord" (2 Corinthians 3:18).

"Sanctify them through thy truth: thy word is truth" (St. John 17:17).

"And be not conformed to this world: but be ye transformed by the renewing of your mind, that ye may prove what is that good, and acceptable, and perfect, will of God" (Romans 12:2).

As you practice being a keen listener, you will become more familiar with God's voice through personal experience. Do nothing without first asking God about it. Seek to involve Him in everything you do. Once you actively involve God in your life, He will be the source, guide, and sustenance of all other relationships. He will put the right people in your path at the right time to take you where He wants you to be. While God will not tell you everything, He will be your guide if you involve Him. We relate to a person based on our involvement with them, and so too it is with God. God reveals His secrets to those who are close to Him.

"The secret of the LORD is with them that fear

Him; and He will shew them His covenant" (Psalm 25:14).

When we examine the life of Christ, we see that His entire life was about love. It was love that led Him to the cross; it was love that led Him to give His life for us; it was love that led Him to give us a second chance. God's secret was love.

The Bible declares that *"Love covers a multitude of sin,"* and His love has covered it all for us. Our duty now is to learn how to abide in His love as His children.

> *"He that dwelleth in the secret place of the most High shall abide under the shadow of the Almighty" (Psalm 91:1).*

The secret place of the Most High is LOVE, and the shadow of the Almighty refers to God's presence, which protects. Once we learn to walk and remain in love, we will have His presence with us in a profound way, always.

We need to learn how to get to that place of love. Our deliverance is hidden in love; our breakthrough lies in love; our healing depends on love; our power and effectiveness are tied to love; the success of our entire lives depends on how we embrace love. We cannot claim to love God without loving others, nor can we love God without a desire to please Him.

Since God is love, it takes God's love to flow through us —our love is temporary, but God's love is eternal.

> *"If ye love me, keep my commandments"* (St. John 14:15).

> *"If ye keep my commandments, ye shall abide in my love; even as I have kept my Father's commandments, and abide in His love. These things have I spoken unto you, that my joy might remain in you, and that your joy might be full. This is my commandment, that ye love one another, as I have loved you. Greater love hath no man than this that a man lay down his life for his friends. Ye are my friends, if ye do whatsoever I command you"* (St. John 15: 10-14).

> *"If a man says, I love God, and hateth his brother, he is a liar: for he that loveth not his brother whom he hath seen, how can he love God whom he hath not seen? And this commandment have we from Him, that he who loveth God love his brother also"* (1 John 4: 20-21).

> *"For all the law is fulfilled in one word, even in this; Thou shalt love thy neighbor as thyself"* (Galatians 5:14).

Love is an action word. Therefore, if we say we love God, we must be doers of the Word and not hearers only.

> *"But whoso hath this world's good, and seeth his brother has need, and shutteth up his bowels of compassion from him, how dwelleth the love of God in him?*
> *My little children, let us not love in word, neither in tongue; but in deed and in truth"* (1 John 3: 17-18).

> *"But be ye doers of the word, and not hearers only, deceiving your own selves"* (James 1:22).

Another meaningful scripture passage, one of my favorites, comes from St. John, chapter fourteen.

> *"He that hath my commandments, and keepeth them, he it is that loveth me: and he that loveth me shall be loved of my Father, and I will love him, and will manifest myself to him.*
> *Judas saith unto him, not Iscariot, Lord, how is it that thou wilt manifest thyself unto us, and not unto the world?*
> *Jesus answered and said unto him, if a man loves me, he will keep my words: and my Father will love him, and we will come unto him, and make our abode with him"* (St. John 14: 21-23).

What power! When we walk in love, it will become evident. When we learn to abide in HIS truth, our entire world and the things around us will change. This is what we need. We need a deep love for God and His Word (the Word is God) to fuel our focus, not just to want Him more, but to do whatever it takes to experience Him in all His fullness. Even when it gets hard, we will honor His Word because we love Him. If we get discouraged along the way, the fear of the Lord will propel us to do what is right, no matter what it costs. If it means that we lose our friends, our family, or other loved ones, we will still be willing to maintain our focus to serve God because of the burning desire within us to please Him.

This newfound love for God will bring a passion for obedience to His Word and for living pure before Him. The desire to serve Him genuinely, hating sin and its very appearance, will be yours. This love will cause you to yearn for His presence – and for more of Him as He begins to reveal Himself to you – leading you to seek Him earnestly, always desiring more.

This is where we will make it all about Him, not about ourselves. His ways will become familiar to us, His desires will become ours, and we will find ourselves wanting to please Him more and more.

When God reveals Himself to us, we will begin to see ourselves as we truly are, recognizing how much we need Him and the love He has for us.

*"For every one that doeth evil hateth the light,
neither cometh to the light, lest his deeds should be
reproved.
But he that doeth truth cometh to the light, that his
deeds may be made manifest, that they are wrought
in God"* (St. John 3: 20-21).

*"As many as I love, I rebuke and chasten: be zealous
therefore, and repent.
Behold, I stand at the door, and knock: if any man
hears my voice, and open the door, I will come in to
him, and will sup with him, and he with me"*
(Revelation 3: 19-20).

A relationship with God is like a series of ongoing revelations. You can't be close to God and stay the same. God seeks genuine fellowship with His followers. Anything hidden in darkness will be exposed by Him in our lives. Nothing will stay concealed when He chooses to reveal it. Are you ready to listen and develop a friendship with Him? Success is within your reach.

Other scripture references:

2 Corinthians 3: 1-18
Colossians 3:25

Philippians 3: 1-21
1 Timothy 4: 1-16

TIMELY THOUGHTS

- Be careful about your beliefs. Not everything you believe to be true is true.
- Man's love has an end, but God's love is eternal.
- God is watching, even when no one else is.
- Whose voice are you listening to?

3
PURITY ROAD

"Blessed are the pure in heart: for they shall see God" (St. Matthew 5:8).

"...present your bodies a living sacrifice; holy, acceptable unto God, which is your reasonable service" (Romans 12:1).

A pure spirit is a free spirit, and only those who are pure will see God. This is serious.

Living in today's world, which is heavily demonized and inhabited by people from diverse backgrounds with varying perspectives, makes it quite challenging to keep a pure spirit. Our physical nature also complicates the struggle against sin, especially those subtle sins we might dismiss as acceptable, even though they are not. Paul shared a bit of his experience on this issue.

> *"For the good that I would I do not: but the evil which I would not, that I do.*
> *Now if I do that I would not, it is no more I that do it, but sin that dwelleth in me"* (Romans 7:19-20).

I really appreciate Paul's honesty. Many people today seek a closer relationship with God, but due to limited understanding and incorrect beliefs—such as expecting to reach a point where fleshly challenges cease—they often become discouraged when caught off guard or tested. Although Paul was a powerful man of God, he still faced daily struggles in his flesh. He knew that to achieve victory, he had to die daily to his soulish desires, not just once. Each new day presented a fresh opportunity, and Paul's victory was secured in his mind.

The main point is to avoid becoming complacent with allowing your flesh to control you. We need to constantly work on maintaining control over our words, actions, and thoughts. This is a continuous journey, and with practice and persistence, our spirits will gradually become more receptive to spiritual matters over time.

If we were alone in this world or could always get our way, life would be less challenging, though not without sin. What I mean is, every day we encounter various people with different beliefs and opinions—leading to conflicts, offenses, and strife—all of which can harm our spirit and inflate our hearts.

We must acknowledge that living this life independently of God is impossible. We need His guidance constantly to lead us into all truth, particularly in areas where we are unaware. To see God's face, we must stay pure before Him, a truth that should motivate us to deepen our relationship with Him. The thought of life without Christ is truly frightening.

Before I delve into what I'll call the purification process, allow me to explain something crucial.

In the book of Genesis, we see that man was created without sin. The love God has for man is profound, and the absence of sin made it possible for God to come down from His throne to commune with mankind. We were created in God's image and likeness, and God values fellowship with man. However, sin has ruined this intimate fellowship, but Jesus' blood has paved a new path, providing restoration. The choice is ours to receive.

"Come now, and let us reason together, saith the Lord: though your sins be as scarlet, they shall be as white as snow; though they be red like crimson, they shall be as wool" (Isaiah 1:18).

"And if it seem evil unto you to serve the Lord,

> *choose you this day whom ye will serve; whether the gods which your fathers served that were on the other side of the flood, or the gods of the Amorites, in whose land ye dwell: but as for me and my house, we will serve the Lord"* (Joshua 24:15).

The cross of Jesus has provided a way for us to no longer remain separated from God and His presence. God loves us so much that He gave His Son's life as a ransom for you and me. Oh, how precious. Sin messed everything up, but God's love restored us. God hates sin; He cannot look upon it. But if we humble ourselves and turn to God with a genuine heart, He will hear us.

> *"The sacrifices of God are a broken spirit: a broken and a contrite heart, O God, thou wilt not despise"* (Psalm 54:17).

> *"The Lord is nigh unto them that are of a broken heart; and saveth such as be of a contrite spirit"* (Psalm 34:18).

How much of God you will have in your life depends on how much of yourself you are willing to deny. How much of His presence you will experience is determined by how obedient you are to Him.

Having the raw evidence of God in your life depends

on how pure you are willing to live for Him. How much of God do you want in your life?

"He must increase, but I must decrease" (St. John 3:30).

God made us with five senses (touch/feel, smell, taste, hearing, and sight), all of which are natural, but the devil often tries to manipulate us through our senses to lure us into sin through deception. Even so, God has given us emotions and feelings, and while some of these feelings may be natural, if we are not careful, we can be subtly led into sin without realizing it because we have accepted something abnormal as normal.

One must recognize that although our feelings and emotions are natural, demonic spirits, which are external entities, can manipulate us through our emotions if an opportunity presents itself. If we are unaware of this deception, acceptance of certain habitual actions, attitudes, feelings, and practices will turn into strongholds.

A stronghold is a demonic hook or grip that a spirit may have over an individual's flesh. A stronghold begins with one thought and grows through our thought patterns and practices. Strongholds act as barriers between God and us, preventing us from gaining complete access to God and the things He has for us. In other words, a stronghold is a strategy or trap that the devil uses against us to divert us, slow us down, or, in some cases, halt our progression and growth in God.

Hurt is a common emotion that the devil uses against us (a feeling). It is almost impossible not to get hurt, and if this feeling is not handled correctly, it will lead to a host of other problems. Our entire lives could change drastically because of one thing, one event, or one person who has caused us pain. Let me give a few examples.

* Peter is having a good day at work. He is the boss's favorite and thinks he is next in line for a promotion. He's on cloud nine until he discovers someone else was promoted in his place. Natural feelings in this scenario could include shock, disappointment, disbelief, and embarrassment (if he was bragging about his impending promotion), but look at what usually happens.

As reality slowly sinks in, you may find that Peter begins to struggle with malice, bitterness, covetousness, a sense of rejection, and more, depending on how he chooses to deal with his disappointment. If Peter is a young Christian, he may easily give in as these spirits persist in trying to take advantage of the situation. A more mature Christian would also experience a struggle, but there would be some resistance, to varying degrees, as long as the person remains alert and watchful in Spirit. Let's look at another example.

* Jane plans a surprise party for her husband and invites a few friends. She is pretty excited and happy with the outcome, but later discovers that her friends are criticizing both her and the event. She feels hurt and decides to confront them. The more she thinks about it, the more hurt she feels, and her hurt quickly turns into anger, puffiness, reservation, and more. Let me share one more example.

* Tom's brother was brutally murdered, but the perpetrator was caught and sent to prison. When Tom first heard of his brother's death, he became very angry, bitter, and vengeful. Even after the killer was caught and sent to prison, Tom's bitterness, hatred, and vengefulness increased. He hopes his brother's killer rots in jail for life if he is not given the death penalty.

One may say these emotions are all natural, and I agree to a certain extent, but it will always remain Tom's responsibility to take control of his feelings by using the Word of God so that demonic spirits gain no advantage from his situation.

Hurt is a natural emotion, but from hurt spring fear, envy, rebellion, lies, murder, bitterness, anger, and so much more. The devil will use any and every opportunity he gets to try to destroy us. Shortly after an offense, demonic spirits will be present, knocking on your heart's door to gain leverage. It is your choice to open your heart and let them in or to resist these spirits, so they leave, as the Scripture says. Different people handle things differently, but the process we face is similar.

"When the unclean spirit is gone out of a man, he walketh through dry places, seeking rest, and findeth none.
Then he saith, I will return into my house from whence I came out; and when he is come, he findeth it empty, swept, and garnished.
Then goeth he, and taketh with himself seven other spirits more wicked than himself, and they enter in and dwell there: and the last state of that man is worse than the first. Even so shall it be also unto this wicked generation" (Matthew 12:43-45).

"Submit yourselves therefore to God. Resist the devil, and he will flee from you" (James 4:7).

We must examine ourselves daily.

"Examine yourselves, whether ye be in the faith; prove your own selves. Know ye not your own selves, how that Jesus Christ is in you, except ye be reprobates" (2 Corinthians 13:5)?

Peter and Paul talk about the putting on and the putting off of these things, and this is what the purification process is all about.

According to www.dictionary.reference.com, the word 'purify' means to make pure; free from anything that debases, pollutes, adulterates, or contaminates. Another meaning is to be free from foreign, extraneous, or objectionable elements.

In simple terms, it is our responsibility as Children of God to ensure that nothing outside of God is found within us. God does the purifying, but it will always remain our responsibility to yield ourselves to Him and to whatever process He sees fit to carry us through.

The purification process entails a sincere search for God. It reflects our total dependence on God for Him to show us ourselves. It involves tearing down and removing every wall or barrier created in our lives over the years, emotionally, mentally, socially, spiritually, and physically, as necessary. It entails the removal of self; the circumcision of the heart; and the transformation or renewal of one's mind and behavioral practices in accordance with the Word of God. It is where we begin to read the Word of God and gain an understanding of His Word sufficient to provoke us to live it out in every way possible. It is all about acquiring a heart fully turned toward God.

I believe the most difficult part of being a Child of God is acquiring and maintaining a pure heart (maintenance is more difficult). Maintaining a pure heart requires every effort on our part, and this is probably the most tedious thing a Christian may have to endure (besides persecution – the giving of one's life for the sake of the gospel), and also gaining control of our minds.

> *"Do ye think that the scripture saith in vain, the spirit that dwelleth in us lusteth to envy"* (James 4:5)?

A constant war rages within us. The moment we lower our guard may be the moment spirits walk in to invade our lives. They are constantly knocking and looking for an opportune time to enter.

Only those with a pure heart will see God. Take a moment to reflect on yourself. The opposite of a pure heart is a corrupt, dirty, filthy, unclean, or unwashed heart. By unwashed, I do not refer to those who are not saved, because many Believers still have an evil and unrepentant heart. Your heart can be either clean or unclean, but it can't be both at the same time. Please reflect on your present state. Do you struggle with unforgiveness, hatred, envy, strife, rebellion, bitterness, or lust, just to name a few? Are you proud or scornful? If you have answered yes to any of these, you have a corrupt heart, and that is the manifestation of the flesh in your life. Repent now and ask God for His cleansing before evil spirits invade your life.

Let's look at the word pure. According to the Oxford Dictionary, the word pure means clean, free from evil, not mixed with anything else, complete, and thorough.

The Greek word for pure is 'Hagos,' meaning pure from defilement, not contaminated, and holy. Does any of this sound familiar? No wonder God calls us to be separated from the world and to live holy lives as He is holy. Our hearts need to be circumcised daily by the Word of God.

> *"Wherefore come out from among them, and be ye separate, saith the Lord, and touch not the unclean thing; and I will receive you"* (2 Corinthians 6:17),

> *"For I am the LORD that bringeth you up out of the land of Egypt, to be your God: ye shall therefore be holy, for I am holy* (Leviticus 11:45).

The only way to acquire a pure heart is to go through the purification process in brokenness and sincere humility before God. There is no way around it but to be purged.

Our experiences of purification may be different, but we all go through the same process. We all have our own struggles, and the length of the process depends entirely on how humble and how aware we are of what is happening in our lives. The sooner we yield to God or the sooner we get it, the sooner the process will end.

I find it very interesting that whatever is lacking in our lives is also required for wholeness. Whatever we are found wanting when we are weighed in the balance will be needed for completion. So, if you find you lack patience and are praying about it, you can expect situations to arise that test it. If you lack peace, you will be placed in situations that call for peace, so that you can become the character of peace. If you are a proud person, God will humble you by allowing you to experience undesirable circumstances. If you struggle with unforgiveness, whether you recognize it or not, God may allow you to be placed in a situation where you learn to forgive.

Sometimes we will never know what is in us until we face certain challenges. Whatever you fall short of, God will bring it to you to replace what is lacking. God knows how to get our attention and to enforce His principles.

The aim of the purification process is to conform us to Christ, enabling us to live a selfless life in obedience to God. If you have a need for change, God will not come down and change you, but He will always provide an opportunity for you to change. The purification process is grounded in these principles.

The Process of Purification

See yourself through God's Word and recognize the need for change: the Word of God serves as a mirror, showing us who we are. The more we study the Word of God, the more clearly we will see ourselves, including how far or how close we are to God. The Word of God sanctifies, cleanses, renews, refreshes, revives, restores, directs, and instructs. It is the truth, and when applied, it changes our hearts.

"The words of the LORD are pure words: as silver tried in a furnace of earth, purified seven times" (Psalm 12:6).

"Sanctify them through thy truth: thy word is truth" (St. John 17:17).

Expect trials in order to overcome: Almost every scripture that speaks of purification also speaks of being tried. Trials are a critical part of the purification process, so knowledge and awareness are crucial. Prepare yourself for trials and be aware, because it is not a matter of if you will be tried, but when.

To qualify for the blessing, you must first pass your test. Think of it as an exam. You will not pass the test until you study and gain the required knowledge, and you will not be qualified to receive your reward until you sit for the exam and pass it. Whenever a student is being taught, the teacher is usually interactive and responsive in class, but when test time arrives, the teacher becomes silent, and interaction is restricted. The same applies to our lives. We can know when a test is in session because this is when we often hear God less, if we even hear Him at all. You know those moments when you may begin to wonder, does God care? Or, is He even there? Never mistake God's silence for absence. He is there overseeing the entire process. Just remember, it is only a test. Feed on the Word of God so that when trials come, you will be strong enough to face your challenges and overcome.

> *"Beloved, think it not strange concerning the fiery trial which is to try you, as though some strange thing happened unto you"* (1 Peter 4:12):

> *"Every man's work shall be made manifest: for the day shall declare it, because it shall be revealed by fire; and the fire shall try every man's work of what sort it is"* (1 Corinthians 3:13).

> *"Wherein ye greatly rejoice, though now for a season, if need be, ye are in heaviness through manifold temptations: That the trial of your faith, being much more precious than of gold that perisheth, though it be tried with fire, might be found unto praise and honor and glory at the appearing of Jesus Christ"* (1 Peter 1:6-7):

"Woe unto him that striveth with his Maker! Let the potsherd strive with the potsherds of the earth. Shall the clay say to him that fashioneth it, what makest thou? Or thy work, He hath no hands" (Isaiah 45:9)?

"And I will bring the third part through the fire, and

will refine them as silver is refined, and will try them as gold is tried: they shall call on my name, and I will hear them: I will say, It is my people: and they shall say, The LORD is my God" (Zachariah 13:9).

Maintenance: This is where the victory is, at the hardest part, when you may feel like giving up. It is never easy to love your enemies, do well to those who hate you, bless those who curse you, or to pray for those who spitefully use you, but we must. Even when it seems as though you have to do good too often for those who treat you badly, you must continue to pursue righteousness and abstain from evil, such as hating those who hate you.

Think of it as a woman who is pregnant. When the time comes for her to give birth, you will find that the baby, who is considered the joy of the journey or the gift desired, comes with pain. During those moments of pain, the expectant mother is expected to push – not when she feels like it or when the pain subsides, but during the pain. The baby cannot come without those pains, nor can the mother push without pain, because it is the pain that assists in pushing the baby down the birth canal and eventually out. Whenever there is no pain, the baby becomes stagnant, but as soon as the pain resumes, the contractions that cause the pain begin to propel the baby further down the birth canal, and the mother is then expected to assist by pushing.

If the mother refuses to push during contractions, the birthing process will be interrupted, and complications may develop, even to the point of death.

Whenever the Lord wants to bless us, the process is similar. It is easy for people to do what they know they must when they feel good, but the most important time to do what is right is in difficult times, when we do not feel like it. New life comes through pain. It is through pain that many dreams, assignments, and discoveries unfold. Success is born in pain. If you refuse to push through the pain and hardship and to do what is right – even in the midst of tragedy – you will not reap your reward. Do not allow your purpose and your blessings to be aborted. Focus and push with everything you have, because situations are only temporary. They won't last.

When you push yourself to go all out and do what is right to please God, everything about you will change because God will visit you. He will draw closer to you as you draw closer to Him, and your eyes will begin to open to a new dimension and a different realm as God elevates you. You will begin to see things differently from that elevated position, and you will experience victory after victory. You will move from one level to the next and from glory to glory, as Paul states it. This stage calls us to become more practical as we see real results and begin to discover God in a whole new way, as He truly is. If you want to experience God's presence, become a doer of the

Word. If you want to experience more of God, get radical and commit to obedience; always strive to do what is right. If you want to know God in all His fullness, continue on this path, and you will discover more and more as you progress on your journey. This is guaranteed!

> *"My brethren, count it all joy when ye fall into divers temptations;*
> *Knowing this, that the trying of your faith worketh patience.*
> *But let patience have her perfect work, that ye may be perfect and entire, wanting nothing" (James 1:2-4).*

> *"But if ye have bitter envying and strife in your hearts, glory not, and lie not against the truth.*
> *This wisdom descendeth not from above, but is earthly, sensual, devilish.*
> *For where envying and strife is, there is confusion and every evil work" (James 3:14-16).*

> *"Wherefore laying aside all malice, and all guile, and hypocrisies, and envies, and all evil speakings,*
> *As newborn babes, desire the sincere milk of the word that ye may grow thereby:*
> *If so be ye have tasted that the Lord is gracious" (1 Peter 2:1-3).*

"But now ye also put off all these; anger, wrath, malice, blasphemy, filthy communication out of your mouth.
Lie not one to another, seeing that ye have put off the old man with his deeds;
And have put on the new man, which is renewed in knowledge after the image of Him that created him"
(Colossians 3:8-10):

"But we all, with open face beholding as in a glass the glory of the Lord, are changed into the same image from glory to glory, even as by the Spirit of the Lord" (2 Corinthians 3:18).

"For whatsoever is born of God overcometh the world: and this is the victory that overcometh the world, even our faith" (1 John 5:4).

"Now the works of the flesh are manifest, which are these; Adultery, fornication, uncleanness, lasciviousness,
Idolatry, witchcraft, hatred, variance, emulations, wrath, strife, seditions, heresies,
Envyings, murders, drunkenness, revellings, and such like: of the which I tell you before, as I have also told you in time past, that they which do such

things shall not inherit the Kingdom of God"
(Galatians 5:19-21).

Galatians 5:19-21 tells us that if we do not learn to mortify the deeds of the flesh by putting our flesh under subjection, we will not inherit the Kingdom of God. This is the reason we do what we do – to see God. The devil was kicked out of heaven because of a heart condition caused by pride. Can you identify any heart condition in your life right now?

This is hard work, though it becomes easier over time (after consistently putting the Word of God into practice). The question you really need to ask yourself to get going is, where do you want to spend your eternity, in hell or in heaven?

"Let no man despise thy youth; but be thou an example of the Believers, in word, in conversation, in charity, in spirit, in faith, in purity" (1 Timothy 4:12).

"Beloved, now are we the sons of God, and it doth not yet appear what we shall be: but we know that, when He shall appear, we shall be like Him; for we shall see Him as He is.
And every man that hath this hope in Him purifieth himself, even as He is pure" (1 John 3: 2-3).

> *"Having therefore these promises, dearly beloved, let us cleanse ourselves from all filthiness of the flesh and spirit, perfecting holiness in the fear of God"* (2 Corinthians 7:1).

> *"Fight the good fight of faith, lay hold on eternal life, whereunto thou art also called, and hast professed a good profession before many witnesses"* (1 Timothy 6:12).

God is coming back for a spotless church. I implore you to get practical, become a doer, and remain faithful to God's Word.

In Esther's story, virgins underwent a year of purification—six months bathing in myrrh oil and another six months with sweet fragrances—before appearing before the king. This illustrates how much more we should continually cleanse ourselves and allow God to refine us through His Word. By reading, meditating, and living righteously, we ensure that our lives emit a pleasing aroma before Him. We are called to distance ourselves from anything that pollutes, corrupts, or contaminates, so that our sacrificial lives become a fragrant offering to God.

One day, at the end of your process, God will show up. Once you remain constant, He will show up! Like the baths in oil and myrrh followed by sweet odors, this will be a bittersweet experience for us. Things may be bitter at first, but if you are willing to hold on to the end, I assure you, it will become sweet eventually.

Every person has a spirit, every spirit carries a presence, and every presence has a smell (like attracts like). If you walk around with malice, hatred, and unforgiveness, you will only attract negative forces to yourself. On the other hand, when you carry the smell of holiness, righteousness, and cleanliness, you will attract God to yourself and to your situation. The smell of righteousness will literally pull God toward you like a magnet, and this is how you will attract His presence.

Have you ever been in a room where the entire atmosphere changed after someone stepped in? Or have you ever been able to tell when a particular person entered a room without first seeing them? This is because of the scent and the presence they carry.

What kind of spirit do you embody, and what scent do you carry? Are you conscious of the spirits you attract each day?

Walk faithfully before the King of kings and keep yourselves pure, reflecting obedience and reverence. He sacrificed His life for us, and our best response is to maintain a sincere heart and spirit to please God.

"Forasmuch then as Christ hath suffered for us in the flesh, arm yourselves likewise with the same

mind: for he that hath suffered in the flesh hath ceased from sin;
That he no longer should live the rest of his time in the flesh to the lusts of men, but to the will of God"
(1 Peter 4:1-2).

"Be sober, be vigilant; because your adversary the devil, as a roaring lion, walketh about, seeking whom he may devour" (1 Peter 5:8):

"Let the word of Christ dwell in you richly in all wisdom; teaching and admonishing one another in psalms and hymns and spiritual songs, singing with grace in your hearts to the Lord" (Colossians 3:16).

Other Scripture references:

Colossians 3:1-17
Jeremiah 18:1-4
Joshua 6 & 7
Numbers 33:50-56
Romans 12:2

TIMELY THOUGHTS

- Only the pure in heart will see God.
- Every person has a spirit; every spirit carries a presence, and every presence has a scent. What scent are you carrying?
- God desires for us to live in such a way that nothing of the devil is found within us.
- God wants our whole hearts, not just a part.
- Circumcision of the heart - the cutting away of the flesh hurts, but the process is necessary.
- New life comes through pain; focus and push. Give birth to your destiny.

4
THE ROAD OF FREEDOM

"...let us lay aside every weight, and the sin which doth so easily beset us, and let us run with patience the race that is set before us,
Looking unto Jesus, the author and finisher of our faith, who for the joy that was set before him endured the cross, despising the shame, and is set down at the right hand of the throne of God"
(Hebrews 12:1-2).

"Casting all your care upon Him; for He careth for you" (1 Peter 5:7).

One of the most valuable steps we can take for ourselves is to let go of baggage. Although it sounds simple, it can be quite challenging. In chapter one, the emphasis was on God, but in this chapter, we'll shift focus to ourselves while keeping God in mind—we can never exclude Him from the process. We always need God to guide and support us. Ultimately, it is through God that we can truly see ourselves.

We must realize that we are in a daily fight, but this is also a race. This is a race for our souls, as the devil recognizes that time is running out. I love how Paul puts it. Paul says, "Lay aside every weight," and then goes on to say, "running this race with patience." If you look into it, running with weights is more difficult than running without them. Your load determines the level of difficulty, and it can easily lead to frustration, causing you to give up, become stagnant, or get stuck in a state of perplexity. This is why patience and knowledge are needed.

You would be surprised by how people respond differently to things they are aware of compared to what they remain ignorant of. Often, the desire to approach situations differently exists but seems almost impossible, because the knowledge of how to do it differently is missing—after all, you can't do something effectively if you don't know how.

Your past can affect you throughout your lifetime if you allow it, and it can even control you if you fail to recognize it. Let's face it. No one was born into a stable relationship with God. The things we know now, we did not know then, so the chances of us dealing with hurts inappropriately in the past are huge.

For many people, memories of the past remain and carry with them lingering pain. Although these memories might not be at the forefront all the time, their impact can be long-lasting. Your capacity to make sound decisions might be compromised when your judgment is clouded by fear, sometimes without your awareness.

A common example involves someone whose heart has been broken and who decides—whether consciously or unconsciously—to never love again. Some individuals remain aware of this choice, while others continue to drift through multiple relationships, often ending in disappointment, driven by a deep-seated fear of heartache that they may not even recognize.

This applies to those afraid of commitment as well; it often stems from fears rooted in a troubled past. If these psychological issues are not addressed promptly, they can become ingrained in your personality. With God's help, they can be eradicated, but the longer they go unexamined, the more difficult it becomes to identify and resolve them. Therefore, it's crucial to regularly reflect on ourselves and to release any unwanted traits or fears, so our past does not control our future. This self-awareness is vital for achieving success.

Many people carry significant emotional baggage, and I can speak from experience, having had too much of it myself. The scars from a painful past can be surprisingly influential. I tended to turn everything in my environment into negativity. For example, if I failed at something, my subconscious would convince me I was unworthy of anyone's love, without me even realizing it. Similarly, when someone close to me raised their voice, I'd interpret it as a sign of not being loved. Ironically, that was shaped by my own love language.

You see, every typical girl admires her father, and a father's love is significant. I can guarantee you that a girl will look for traits of her father in her spouse. In my case, my father was soft-spoken, and I interpreted that as love. Anything outside of tenderness was not love in my eyes. I was not yet convinced of tough love – the good kind that firmly tries to bring out the best in you (God deals with us tough sometimes for our own good, doesn't He?). I continued to live like this (restricted and limited thinking) for many years, in a world of rejection I created for myself by buying into lies the devil sold me, simply because I was ignorant of what was happening, and I lived a good portion of my life like this.

If you've been following me so far, then I'm sure you've guessed right. For years, I walked around trying to please everyone and prove myself to people, and I also struggled with my self-worth – trying to feel good about myself while seeking approval and acceptance. I valued myself. I knew I was a good person, but I failed to believe anyone knew it. This focus trapped me in a world all by myself and made me quiet, withdrawn, shy, insecure, fearful, and defensive, just to name a few. In short, I became selfish, and all my thoughts, decisions, actions, and attitude were centered on me, based on how I felt and what I was going through at that moment.

I built a life for years around something I made factual, except it never truly was. I am tempted to say 'what wasted years,' but the truth is, I thank God for all those experiences and all the pain that came with them, because I am who I am today because of them. The knowledge and training I have been empowered with by the Holy Spirit have shaped my life in such a way that I would not trade all those hurts, both false and real, for anything else. My past experiences are the core of why I can talk to you this way right now.

The moment you make a conscious decision to change what needs to be changed and remove what needs to go, you can look out for the devil because he will try to stop you in every way possible. The devil knows the seriousness of knowledge, so he will try to keep you in darkness and in bondage. There is power in freedom, so watch out for those false seeds he will try to plant into your mind; seeds of doubt, loneliness, and the belief that you are not valuable or worthy of love. Watch out for those seeds that will make you feel as though the whole world is against you, and you are all alone. It is a trap! And most of the time, it is all lies!

The reality is that not everyone will like you, but not everyone will hate you either. Not everyone will always be pleased with you, but that is life. Learn to distinguish between the truth and reality. While there may be things about you that seem intimidating or that not everyone likes, that does not mean you are not loved or will not be accepted as a person. To be real, however, if you have a bad attitude, it is your attitude that will not be liked, not you.

To demonstrate this, try changing any aspect of yourself that you or others dislike and observe the difference. If the complaint is genuine, this adjustment will likely elicit a positive response. There are always reasons behind people's behavior towards you, as everyone perceives things differently. For example, someone might seem more friendly to others because you appear serious, no-nonsense, or even a bit intimidating for some reason. Perhaps your quiet, reserved nature causes others to think you're not interested, even though that's not true. Consequently, people tend to feel more comfortable with those they perceive as approachable, welcoming, and warm.

Many factors shape how people treat us regularly, beyond the lies the devil may try to deceive you with. Instead of complaining about being disliked, reflect on your actions to see how you might be pushing others away. Self-awareness can lead to change. Perform a soul-search to identify any attitudes that need correction. Remember, you are not the only one facing issues. Sometimes, others' behavior isn't about you, but their own struggles. Be cautious in interpretation; knowledge is power. The world is full of hurting people, and a negative response from someone might be due to their situation, not you. Don't take everything personally, as not everything is about you.

> *"My people are destroyed for lack of knowledge: because thou hast rejected knowledge, I will also reject thee, that thou shalt be no priest to me: seeing thou hast forgotten the law of thy God, I will also forget thy children"* (Hosea 4:6).

People carry emotional baggage from experiences such as a failed marriage or relationship, abuse—whether mental, emotional, spiritual, social, physical, or sexual, including rape, incest, and molestation—the death or loss of a loved one, neglect, unfair or cruel treatment, and other events that cause trauma or pain.

The effects of pain can be quite burdensome, and I listed a few ways we can be negatively affected in the previous chapter, such as becoming rebellious, stubborn, angry, bitter, fearful, and unforgiving. I also spoke about a few examples in this chapter, such as conforming to the need to please everyone, to prove yourself to everyone, becoming defensive and insecure, developing low self-esteem, and having little or no self-value. Most, if not all, stems from fear. Fear is usually the underlying culprit behind most of these effects.

The sad reality is that the only way to control these negative emotions is to face them. The same way you got in is the same way you will get out. So, if you are fearful of entering a relationship you believe is part of God's plan for your life, the only way to combat that fear is not to run away from it but to submit to the will of God while seeking the courage to stand and face the challenges that may come with it. You need as much of God as you can get for this part of the process. As you release your life and your trust in God, He will give you peace to calm and soothe your fears, and you will be able to see Him at work in you. Things will change in such a way that, when you reflect on your past, you may ask yourself, 'When did I get here?' And what if I had given up? But God cannot help you until you take that first step. That first step can sometimes be the most difficult, though the latter can be great just the same.

Make a conscious decision to break down every barrier in your life by facing your fears. As you do so prayerfully and with total dependence on God, He will help you.

With this being said, focus on God more than on others. Your focus must be entirely on pleasing God, not necessarily on others. Change your priorities and shift your focus. Both you and others will benefit, but do it to please God and because it is the right thing to do. Always keep your motives and priorities in check.

"And whatsoever ye do, do it heartily, as to the Lord, and not unto men" (Colossians 3:23).

"Not with eye service, as men pleasers; but as the servants of Christ, doing the will of God from the heart;
With goodwill doing service, as to the Lord, and not to men" (Ephesians 6:6-7).

The constant need for attention, the desperate need for approval, and the dreaded need for acceptance and affirmation speak volumes. They mirror what is taking place within you. Before you can love others, you must first love yourself. Love begins with you. Take the initiative. If you do not feel good about yourself, no one can fix that for you. You can hide behind the love you receive from people, but that would only offer a temporary fix. If you often feel lonely, sad, hurt, or unhappy, try shifting your attention to yourself and do a 'soul search.' Look deep within yourself rather than looking to others to fix or soothe what is happening inside you. Allow God to heal you. If you cannot learn to make yourself happy, no one will be able to make you happy, and you won't be able to make others happy either. True happiness comes from within, not from without. Accept yourself for who you are so that others can accept you.

If you do not learn to value yourself, people will take

advantage of you. Value yourself so that others will value you. Believe it or not, people will treat you based on the presence you carry. If you walk around feeling less important or insignificant, you will be easily overlooked, but if you work to build your confidence, you will stand out whenever you enter a room. Do not do anything, however, to be seen or to get noticed, but build on the right foundation and act on the Word of God because it is the right thing to do. Believe in yourself, and you will be able to convince others that you have something valuable and special to offer the world. With this assurance, when you walk, walk with the boldness and confidence of accepting God's love and plans for your life, knowing that the Creator of the universe walks with you.

Once you have come to accept God's love for you, it becomes easier to walk in love and to accept the love of others. When you begin to see things the way God sees them, everything will change, even that which seems impossible or difficult. Be happy with who you are. Recognize that this is a process. Just as it took time to get to where you are now, it will take time to get you out of it. Have patience, work hard at it, involve God always, and He will change the things you cannot change on your own. Love God, love yourself, be happy, and do not forget to exercise patience and love others as well.

With all the pressure and demands life brings, walking around trying to gain approval from everyone is the last thing you need. I believe the three main hindrances to revealing one's true self are the constant need to protect oneself from the fear of criticism or failure, the fear of rejection, and the fear of getting hurt. No one likes to fail or get hurt, and people in these categories may be labeled "thin-skinned" or "abnormal," but what I really see are people who have been through a lot and need a little courage, extra support, and reassurance in life.

As you work to break down these barriers, develop an awareness of what you do and why you do it. Monitor your feelings and actions. This will show what is really happening on the inside of you and the progress you are making, if any.

Never compare yourself to others. Do not try to match up with people or their standards. Instead, try to please God and live up to His standards. Quit trying to please everyone. Refuse to live your life based on what people think, because what they think of you does not always matter. Don't give in to urges to prove yourself, especially over petty things. Weaning yourself from unhealthy practices is part of the growth process (becoming a mature Christian).

Let go of those burdens and free yourself from the weight and baggage you now carry. Please don't get me wrong; it is alright to clear your name of something like a false accusation if needed, but if your explanation goes unacknowledged or if things seem as though they could get out of control, resist any unhealthy urge to persist in an effort to defend yourself, especially when it is unnecessary. Leave it to God, and He will fix for you what you can't. Be in control of your feelings, and do not let them control you. You can be recognized by man, but not recognized by God. Whose recognition is more important? Man sees the outside and what you appear to be, but God sees the heart, which shows who you really are. It does not matter what man thinks about you or what they choose to believe; what matters is what God knows and how He sees you.

> *"And it came to pass, when they were come, that he looked on Eliab and said, surely the Lord's anointed is before him.*
> *But the Lord said unto Samuel, look not on his countenance, or on the height of his stature; because I have refused him: for the Lord seeth not as man seeth; for man looketh on the outward appearance, but the Lord looketh on the heart"* (1 Samuels 16:6-7).

Work on doing what is right, no matter what. Replace negativity with positivity, keep a free heart, give everything to God, and say hello to freedom as you pave the way for success and transition into a brand-new you.

. . .

Other Scripture references:

St. Matthew 23
Galatians 6:7-8
Romans 13:1-4

TIMELY THOUGHTS

- Your past can ruin your future if you let it.
- Not every urge is normal; some stem from demonic roots.
- You must be in control of your emotions, not have them control you.
- Instead of making excuses for your actions, acknowledge where you went wrong. That is how you will experience change.
- Something positive can be found in every negative situation.
- Allow things to make you better, not bitter.

5

DETERMINATION DRIVE

"And let us not be weary in well doing: for in due season we shall reap, if we faint not" (Galatians 6:9).

"Withhold not good from them to whom it is due, when it is in the power of thine hand to do it" (Proverbs 3:27).

There are two well-known quotes: "Nothing beats a trial but a failure" and "If at first you don't succeed, try again." Making changes can be difficult, especially in longstanding or deeply rooted situations. However, to achieve victory, you need to stay persistent and consistent in your efforts to attain the results you want. Persistence is essential for success.

Think of it this way: if you want to build muscle and get a toned body, joining a program at first may be inspiring, but after realizing how hard you have to work and how long it will take to get there, it can lead to discouragement.

Just as you cannot get the body you dream of by simply lying on the couch, so too is it with building Godly character and a shapely personality. The reward comes after the work, and though you will encounter difficulty along the way, you need to affirm yourself by saying, 'giving up is not an option.'

Determination is crucial to overcoming stagnation, something we all must recognize—the absence of growth in our lives. The Christian journey focuses on growth. Paul mentions moving from glory to glory, implying maturity, while Peter speaks of newborn babes, illustrating progression through various stages.

> *"As newborn babes, desire the sincere milk of the word that ye may grow thereby"* (1 Peter 2:2):

> *"But we all, with open face beholding as in a glass the glory of the Lord, are changed into the same image from glory to glory, even as by the Spirit of the Lord"* (2 Corinthians 3:18).

> *"And I, brethren, could not speak unto you as unto spiritual, but as unto carnal, even as unto babes in Christ.*
> *I have fed you with milk, and not with meat: for hitherto ye were not able to bear it, neither yet now are ye able"* (1 Corinthians 3:1-2).

It's pointless to persist in something that won't benefit you. Be ready to invest all necessary effort and patience to change or reach your goals. Do what is needed, and never consider your current situation as your final state, regardless of circumstances.

A few scriptures that have helped me along my journey are as follows:

> *"Be not deceived; God is not mocked: for whatsoever a man soweth, that shall he also reap.*
> *For he that soweth to his flesh shall of the flesh reap corruption; but he that soweth to the Spirit shall of the Spirit reap life everlasting.*
> *And let us not be weary in well doing: for in due season we shall reap, if we faint not.*
> *As we have therefore opportunity, let us do good unto all men, especially unto them who are of the household of faith"* (Galatians 6:7-10).

> *"For rulers are not a terror to good works, but to the*

> *evil. Wilt thou then not be afraid of the power? Do that which is good, and thou shalt have praise of the same:*
> *For he is the minister of God to thee for good. But if thou do that which is evil, be afraid; for he beareth not the sword in vain: for he is the minister of God, a revenger to execute wrath upon him that doeth evil"* (Romans 13:3-4).

Did you get that? Now that is frightening! Whatever you do, the same will be measured back to you. If you do what is evil, the Bible tells us to be afraid because it will not go in vain. May God have mercy!

Are you an evil doer? Do you practice doing things that are wrong in the eyes of God? Watch out, because payday is coming. A lot of what we go through in life – believe it or not – is 'payback' for what we have done. If you sow to the flesh, you will reap from the flesh, and if you sow to the spirit, you will reap from the spirit. Whatever you do in life will be measured back to you. So, if you sow mercy, you will receive mercy; if you sow kindness and love, you will reap the same; if you sow forgiveness, you will also receive forgiveness, etc. The opposite holds true as well. If you practice being mean, hateful, impatient, or selfish toward others, you will be storing up for yourself an inheritance despised. Be careful what you do, what you say, and how you treat others, because your reward awaits you. It pays to be good, to do good, and to be consistent in what you do.

God's desire is to bless us continually, but the blessings He has for us cannot flow consistently into our lives until our walk with Him becomes consistent. Many people may only experience raindrops on and off, but God wants to continually pour His blessings upon us.

There are seasons for everything, and the idea is for us to give God free course in our lives so that the only time we may suffer need is when we are tested, if it pleases Him. Whatever happens, it must be that God is in control, not that we are out of alignment or inconsistent in practicing obedience to God's Word.

The devil knows the power of consistency, which is why he will try to distract you with discouragement and frustration. But if you remain faithful to God in all you do, you will reap the reward. Keep going, even when it hurts, and you do not feel like it. Do not settle for less when God is not in it. Go after God with your whole heart, do what is required of you, commit your ways to Him, and you will see the results. Giving up is not an option; do not cease from doing what is right, especially after you begin to reap the rewards.

How much of God do you want? Be determined to adapt to the character of Christ, and every area of your life will be positively affected.

"For God is not unrighteous to forget your work and labor of love, which ye have shewn toward his name, in that ye have ministered to the saints, and do minister" (Hebrews 6:10).

"And as ye would that men should do to you, do ye also to them likewise.
For if ye love them which love you, what thank have ye? For sinners also love those who love them.
And if ye do good to them which do good to you, what thank have ye? For sinners also do even the same.
And if ye lend to them of whom ye hope to receive, what thank have ye? For sinners also lend to sinners, to receive as much again.
But love ye your enemies, and do good, and lend, hoping for nothing again; and your reward shall be great, and ye shall be the children of the Highest: for He is kind unto the unthankful and to the evil.
Be ye therefore merciful, as your Father also is merciful.
Judge not, and ye shall not be judged: condemn not, and ye shall not be condemned: forgive, and ye shall be forgiven:
Give, and it shall be given unto you; good measure, pressed down, and shaken together, and running over, shall men give into your bosom. For with the

same measure that ye mete withal it shall be measured to you again" (St. Luke 6:31-38).

Never focus on how far you have to go to reach where you need to be. Trust God and take it one day at a time. Remember, *"After you endure, you will obtain the promise."* Not before, but AFTER, so it is important to eliminate discouragement and anything that will interfere with your focus or slow your progress by meditating on the Word of God and by channeling your thoughts toward what God says about you through His Word. It does not matter how fast you get there; you just need to ensure you are moving and do not remain in the same position for long. Slow growth is better than stagnation or regression. Take one step at a time, and one day you will fulfill your promise.

The race is not for the swift or the battle for the strong, but for those who can endure to the end. Determination and endurance are important factors in reaping success.

Other Scripture References:

Luke 6: 20-38
Romans 12:18
Philippians 4:13
Colossians 3: 23-24

1 Corinthians 3:7-15
Isaiah 43: 1-19

TIMELY THOUGHTS

- *Giving up is not an option.*
- *Every action has a consequence. Whatever you do will be measured back to you.*
- *Your harvest comes after sowing (doing the work), not before.*
- *Do ALL things wholeheartedly, as unto the Lord.*
- *Persistence is the key to success.*

6
CONFIDENCE AVENUE

"It is better to trust in the Lord than to put confidence in man" (Psalm 118:8).

"I can do all things through Christ who strengthens me" (Philippians 4:13).

Our strength, our help, our source, and our hope are found in God and in Him alone. They are not found in our jobs, our profession, our money, our family, our abilities and talents, nor in earthly possessions or material gains, but in Christ alone. Everything we can ever hope for or imagine; everything we can dream of and will achieve must have God as its source.

God has specific blessings set for us, His children, at specific points throughout our journey, but He wants us to learn to rest in Him and to develop trust while waiting, so that everything can be fulfilled in His timing through our obedience to His Word and our loyalty to Him, demonstrated by our willingness to obey.

It is very easy to place our trust in something or someone outside of Christ without even realizing it. I will share a story of a lesson I was taught about faith. Whenever things went smoothly, I was joyful, but the moment I faced need, I became deeply affected by worry. God knew this, and He decided to teach me a lesson.

My family went through a very trying period when we were literally forced to live one day at a time, and it was a walk by faith. This was hardly a problem for my husband, whom I often teased whenever I referred to him as a 'Man of Faith' or sometimes 'Richey,' because his disposition, by nature, has always been positive, due to the many experiences he gained from being on his own from a very early age, sixteen. I was raised in a sheltered environment and lacked experience, so this was a valuable learning experience for me.

We went down to nothing. We had zero dollars in our bank accounts, but whatever needs we had for that day were met, just in time, not before. Our dinner and all the food we needed for each day were included in this lesson.

At a specific time each day, the exact amount of money needed for the moment, whether to buy food for one day's dinner or to pay a bill that had to be paid at that time – whatever – would be provided. This continued several times throughout each day, based on our needs for the moment, for over one week.

This was one of the most difficult practical lessons I have ever experienced. I was extremely tense throughout the entire process, not knowing what would happen, but the outcome was fruitful. From this experience, I learned that my trust was not really in God but in our money. I became so relaxed whenever money was around, but restless whenever there was none. God is our true provider; He is our source. Therefore, our trust should be in Him alone, not in our money. The lesson He demonstrated in my life confirmed that He is truly a Father who knows how to take care of His children. If we will only trust Him sincerely! What or who do you trust right now? Who do you look to for help? Do you look to your family, your friends, your neighbors, or your spouse? Or is your trust in your money, your abilities, your possessions, or your profession? In whom or what do you put your trust? Please take some time to genuinely think about this.

"Some trust in chariots, and some in horses: but we

> *will remember the name of the LORD our God"*
> *(Psalm 20:7).*

If you are going to build anything, it is best to ensure the foundation is strong. A strong foundation is the root of a strong structure. If a building is not laid on a solid foundation, it will eventually crumble, especially when subjected to pressure or resistance. This same principle applies to our personal lives and growth in Christ. We must build upon a solid foundation.

A solid foundation can only be found in Christ. All other things outside of Christ will vanish, so we must build only upon the truth of His Word.

> *"The grass withereth, the flower fadeth: but the word of our God shall stand for ever" (Isaiah 40:8).*

Everything outside the truth of God's Word will fade and crumble, so we must build on His Word and on truth.

> *"According to the grace of God which is given unto me, as a wise master builder, I have laid the foundation, and another buildeth thereon. But let every man take heed how he buildeth thereupon. For other foundation can no man lay than that is laid, which is Jesus Christ.*

Now if any man builds upon this foundation gold, silver, precious stones, wood, hay, stubble; Every man's work shall be made manifest: for the day shall declare it, because it shall be revealed by fire; and the fire shall try every man's work of what sort it is.
If any man's work abides which he hath built thereupon, he shall receive a reward.
If any man's work shall be burned, he shall suffer loss: but he himself shall be saved; yet so as by fire"
(*1 Corinthians 3:10-15*).

When you decide to face a challenge, make a change, start fresh, or go deeper in God, opposition will come, so you must be prepared to PUSH through the phases of trials, no matter what.

According to Genesis 3:15, which says, *"And I will put enmity between thee and the woman, and between thy seed and her seed; it shall bruise thy head, and thou shall bruise his heel,"* it becomes clear to me that if we hope to accomplish anything at all in life, we must learn to use this simple four-letter word, PUSH.

When I consider the word PUSH, it suggests that something is in front of you. No one needs to push an open door, but a closed door requires forceful effort to open so you can go through and reach the other side.

A lot of things can set us back in life, but we must learn

to push past them. We have to push against negativity, push against distractions, push past discouragement, and push past all else. This is a stage where we must be willing to fight, and if we intend to make heaven our home or to achieve what God has for us, we must PUSH.

It is your duty to pray when you do not feel like it, to love when you are not up to it, to give to those who don't deserve it, and to be kind to those who are cruel to you. Do not worry about feeling like a hypocrite for doing something you have no desire to do. God looks upon the heart, and He judges us based on the sincerity of our hearts. If you genuinely desire to please God and will yourself to do what is not desired but pleasing in His sight, hypocrisy won't be part of the equation. Will yourself to do it until it becomes part of your nature. We all have to start somewhere, and thinking negatively will only hold you back. This is why knowledge is important. There is a vast difference when we fight with knowledge.

If we learn to move beyond our past, overcome diversity and adversity, and persist through hardship and every obstacle in our way, we will truly come to value the rewards of perseverance.

God did not promise us an easy life; He never promised a bed full of roses, but He promised us a life of victory and success if we get used to pushing by being obedient to His Word. How can you experience victory without a trial? Many people want victory without trials.

Many desire to reign with Christ, but no one wants to suffer for Him. Our anointing and our relationship with God do not guarantee that we will be kept out of trouble, but they will protect and guide us in times of trouble. Daniel was delivered not from the lion's den, but OUT of the lion's den. The three Hebrew boys were not delivered from the fire, but OUT of the fire. Joseph was not delivered from the hands of his brothers or from the mouth of Potiphar's wife, but he was eventually exalted. Wherever he went, favor followed him, because God was with him.

Change is not easy, and the challenges are tough, but the only way to overcome them is to stand up to your opponent and do what is right in the sight of God (whether you feel like it or not); you must take a stand for what is right and fight.

> *"Be not overcome by evil, but overcome evil with good (Romans 21:21).*

All of this cannot be done in your own strength; it will take the strength of God and His help, along with much effort on your part. So, remain determined and confident until change comes.

> *"And why call ye me, Lord, Lord, and do not the things which I say?*

Whosoever cometh to me, and heareth my sayings, and doeth them, I will show you to whom he is like: He is like a man who built a house, and dug deep, and laid the foundation on a rock: and when the flood arose, the stream beat vehemently upon that house, and could not shake it: for it was founded upon a rock.
But he that heareth, and doeth not, is like a man that without a foundation built a house upon the earth; against which the stream did beat vehemently, and immediately it fell; and the ruin of that house was great" (St. Luke 6: 46-49).

When I speak of confidence, I do not refer to confidence in your own strengths and abilities, but rather to confidence in God that will then flow into and affect every area of your life. God must be the source of our confidence.

"For in Him we live, and move, and have our being; as certain also of your own poets have said, for we are also his offspring" (Acts 17:28).

King David said -

"Put not your trust in princes, nor in the son of man, in whom there is no help.

> *His breath goeth forth, he returneth to his earth; in that very day his thoughts perish.*
> *Happy is he that hath the God of Jacob for his help, whose hope is in the Lord his God:*
> *Which made heaven, and earth, the sea, and all that therein is: which keepeth truth forever"* (Psalm 146:3-6):

Jeremiah's thoughts on this matter are even more sobering.

> *"Thus, saith the Lord: Cursed be the man that trusteth in man, and maketh flesh his arm, and whose heart departeth from the Lord.*
> *For he shall be like the heath in the desert, and shall not see when good cometh; but shall inhabit the parched places in the wilderness, in a salt land and not inhabited.*
> *Blessed is the man that trusteth in the Lord, and whose hope the Lord is.*
> *For he shall be as a tree planted by the waters, and that spreadeth out her roots by the river, and shall not see when heat cometh, but her leaf shall be green; and shall not be careful in the year of drought, neither shall cease from yielding fruit"* (Jeremiah 17:5-8).

It is easy for us to become dependent on our income, our abilities, and our talents, but may our confidence never be founded in ourselves or in any other; may it be hidden in Christ and rooted only in Him. Our provision is from above, so we must look to God, from whom our help comes.

As you begin to seek God's strength and to become practical by being a doer of the Word of God, you will begin to recognize God's move. This transitional phase will sharpen your faith, deepen your relationship with God, and blossom your confidence as you watch God take the lead in your life. All you have to do is stand still in His presence and allow Him to work through you, but it first requires effort on your part to do what is right, no matter what.

This transitional phase will become your driving force as your desire to know God more increases while you seek Him and remain practical in applying His Word. If you remain focused and sensitive to the pathway of this process, the results will leave you addicted to the Word and doing what is right, enabling you to experience more of Him (this is how you get more).

When you begin to discover that God is more important to you than anyone or anything, and when the foundation is laid so you develop the attitude to do what is right no matter what – even if it costs you your friends or your life – you can rest assured that your confidence in

God is steady. At this point, say hello to a new beginning as you learn to release yourself completely into God's hands.

Confidence in God makes all the difference. It will reorder your priorities, change your thinking, and realign your focus. Everything we need is wrapped up in God and can be found in Him – not in the power of our own hands. This confidence will release assurance and patience, enabling us to hope and trust in God. God knows all things, and there is a time set for us to receive the specific blessings He has for us, but we must be willing to be patient and, like Job, wait for our change. It is dangerous to move outside of God's timing, so I encourage you to hope in God, rest in Him, and wait patiently for Him.

> *"If ye then be risen with Christ, seek those things which are above, where Christ sitteth on the right hand of God.*
> *Set your affection on things above, not on things on the earth.*
> *For ye are dead, and your life is hid with Christ in God"* (Colossians 3:1-3).

> *"Let your conversation be without covetousness; and be content with such things as ye have: for He hath said, I will never leave thee, nor forsake thee"* (Hebrews 13:5).

Confidence in God will give you holy boldness to do as He says and to please Him.

> *"Fear them not therefore: for there is nothing covered, that shall not be revealed; and hid, that shall not be known.*
>
> *What I tell you in darkness, that speak ye in light: and what ye hear in the ear, that preach ye upon the housetops.*
>
> *And fear not them which kill the body, but are not able to kill the soul: but rather fear Him which is able to destroy both soul and body in hell"* (St. Matthew 10:26-28).

> *"Whosoever therefore shall confess me before men, him will I confess also before my Father which is in heaven.*
>
> *But whosoever shall deny me before men, him will I also deny before my Father which is in heaven.*
>
> *Think not that I am come to send peace on earth: I came not to send peace, but a sword.*
>
> *For I am come to set a man at variance against his father, and the daughter against her mother, and the daughter-in-law against her mother-in-law.*
>
> *And a man's foes shall be they of his own household.*
>
> *He that loveth father or mother more than me is not*

*worthy of me: and he that loveth son or daughter
more than me is not worthy of me.
And he that taketh not his cross, and followeth after
me, is not worthy of me"* (St. Matthew 10:32-38).

Oh, may we all reach that place where nothing else matters but God. May our priorities be aligned with God's will, and may our motives be realigned to His Word. May we all reach that place where we are completely sold out to Him – becoming warriors after God's own heart.

Though the source of your confidence must be rooted in God, you also need to come into agreement with God's Word and His promises toward you by believing that God can use you to accomplish His plans, so that the work of God will not be hindered. Even so, this belief is not based on the skills and talents you possess, but rather on Christ and the abilities He has bestowed upon you, so that He can freely do as He pleases in and through you.

Everyone requires confidence, and at some stage in life, it will be tested. Confidence enhances your appearance, making you seem better than you actually are. It gets you noticed, acknowledged, and heard. Confidence produces the boldness needed to take risks. It helps you see what others do not and take bold steps.

Have you ever noticed a hairstyle or outfit so far outside your sense of style that you wouldn't want to be seen wearing it, yet you notice something about the person wearing it that makes you think, "That's pretty cool"? Or have you ever been in a room with people when someone walks in, and all the heads turn because of the energy the person brings, along with their look and walk, making you wonder, "Who is that?" Well, this is the sort of reaction that confidence brings, and it is very much needed in every believer's walk with Christ.

Confidence is having faith or complete trust in someone or something. Allow God to be the source of your faith, as He is the giver and sustainer of life, including your abilities. Trust Him to help you make the most of your abilities and your life. If your confidence is founded on this basis, you will have confidence for a lifetime.

Confidence founded outside of this, within yourself, or in the things you possess, can only be short-lived, as we may fail and our abilities may fail, but God never fails.

Confidence paves the way for opportunities, accomplishments, and positive advancements in life. Confidence makes you stand out. It makes you feel free and helps you ward off burdens and negativity that sometimes rise within you. It gives you the strength to endure and the courage to face challenges, never giving up.

When you have this confidence and hope in Christ, you will recognize that there is no need for jealousy or covetousness when others around you may seem blessed, and your life appears the same. You will not be perturbed or disturbed because you will have the full assurance that

"God will work all things together for your good according to His purpose because you love Him." The patience that confidence produces will remind you that He already has a perfect plan and a specific timing for your life.

Confidence will take you places with God. Make the decision to move past the low self-esteem barrier that constantly tries to impede you by being aggressive against everything that resembles negativity. Use the Word of God to build your faith and trust in God. Seek to know God in all His fullness so that you do not live a life that is limited to your demise.

> *"Cast not away therefore your confidence, which hath great recompense of reward.*
> *For ye have need of patience, that, after ye have done the will of God, ye might receive the promise.*
> *For yet a little while, and he that shall come will come, and will not tarry.*
> *Now the just shall live by faith: but if any man draw back, my soul shall have no pleasure in him.*
> *But we are not of them who draw back unto perdition; but of them that believe to the saving of the soul"* (Hebrews 10:32-39).

May you all find God in such a tangible way that, like David, your confidence will be rooted and grounded in God. May Psalm twenty-three become a practical and applicable part of your life on a daily basis throughout your journey to success!

> *"Yea, though I walk through the valley of the shadow of death, I will fear no evil: for thou art with me; thy rod and thy staff they comfort me"* (Psalm 23:4).

> *"The LORD is on my side; I will not fear: what can man do unto me"* (Psalm 118:6)?

What confidence!

Other Scripture References:

Isaiah 31: 1-3
Psalm 73: 25-28
2 Chronicles 32: 1-8
1 Kings 18
Psalm 27

TIMELY THOUGHTS

- Everything you need is in God.
- Your entire world can be transformed by

simply obeying the Word of God and by replacing negativity with positivity.

- Nothing great comes without pain.
- There is good in every situation; learn to recognize it.
- God changes no one except those who accept the opportunity provided for change.
- An opportunity lost may never be regained. Make use of what you have now.
- God must be the source of our confidence.

7
THE CHOICE PATH

"Behold, I set before you this day a blessing and a curse; A blessing, if ye obey the commandments of the Lord your God, which I command you this day: And a curse, if ye will not obey the commandments of the Lord your God, but turn aside out of the way which I command you this day, to go after other gods, which ye have not known" (Deuteronomy 11:26-28).

"I call heaven and earth to record this day against you, that I have set before you life and death, blessing and cursing: therefore, choose life, that both thou and thy seed may live" (Deuteronomy 30:19).

The church is in a compromised state; it has lost its strength because of a persistent demonic slumber that clouds clarity. This is evident because many Believers' lives do not reflect the life God has promised. God's intention is to bless and prosper us in every aspect of our lives. True prosperity extends beyond finances to include mental, physical, emotional, social, and spiritual health. Until you start thriving in all these areas, you have not fully experienced prosperity.

> *"Beloved, I wish above all things that thou mayest prosper and be in health, even as thy soul prospereth"* (3 John 1:2).

We serve a God who truly desires to bless us, but we also serve a God of principles. The requirements for us to be blessed must be met before we can receive the blessing God intends for us. The sad reality is that many Christians are waiting on God for blessings, yet God is waiting on us to align with His Word so He can bless us!

Before water freezes into ice, the temperature must drop to 32°F. This is the freezing point, and anything above it will prevent water from transforming into ice. The same is true for God and us.

For God to bless us, we have to get ourselves right by aligning our lives with the Word of God. We all have the opportunity to do this by examining the choices we make daily. How far you go in life is not determined by God, but by your obedience to Him – the choices you make – and how much of God you will acquire (power) is not

THE CHOICE PATH

determined by Him, but by your daily living, which spells CHOICES.

Every day we make choices, and God has given us the freedom to choose, so it is up to us. However, we will never have what God desires for us until we begin to make wise and godly choices.

God cares more about our hearts and our relationship with Him than about material blessings. While material blessings are temporary, spiritual blessings last forever, which is why God prioritizes getting our spiritual lives right first. He guides us through a process to achieve this. We can choose to cooperate with God and learn what He wants, which is wise, since fighting Him only prolongs the process. Alternatively, we can rebel like the children of Israel and delay our growth. The process continues until we pass the tests and move forward; otherwise, we keep circling back to the starting point, making no progress.

The Scriptures teach us to love God with ALL our hearts (*please refer to "Heart Path" at the beginning of this book for more information*) and to obey His Word. To love God with ALL our hearts means that He will have our hearts ENTIRELY – not just a part of it, but ALL of it – and this will be revealed in the choices we make. Here is what the Bible says about this:

> *"He that hath my commandments, and keepeth them, he it is that loveth me...*

He that loveth me not, keepeth not my saying..." (St. John 14:21, 24).

Deuteronomy chapter six (6) says:

"Now these are the commandments, the statutes, and the judgments, which the LORD your God commanded to teach you, that ye might do them in the land whither ye go to possess it:
That thou mightest fear the LORD thy God, to keep all His statutes and His commandments, which I command thee, thou, and thy son, and thy son's son, all the days of thy life; and that thy days may be prolonged.
Hear therefore, O Israel, and observe to do it; that it may be well with thee, and that ye may increase mightily, as the LORD God of thy fathers hath promised thee, in the land that floweth with milk and honey.
Hear, O Israel: The LORD our God is one LORD: And thou shalt love the LORD thy God with all thine heart, and with all thy soul, and with all thy might.
And these words, which I command thee this day, shall be in thine heart:
And thou shalt teach them diligently unto thy children, and shalt talk of them when thou sittest in

thine house, and when thou walkest by the way, and when thou liest down, and when thou risest up.

And thou shalt bind them for a sign upon thine hand, and they shall be as frontlets between thine eyes.

And thou shalt write them upon the posts of thy house, and on thy gates.

And it shall be, when the Lord thy God shall have brought thee into the land which He swore unto thy fathers, to Abraham, to Isaac, and to Jacob, to give thee great and goodly cities, which thou buildedst not,

And houses full of all good things, which thou filledst not, and wells digged, which thou diggedst not, vineyards and olive trees, which thou plantedst not; when thou shalt have eaten and be full;

Then beware lest thou forget the L<small>ORD</small>, *which brought thee forth out of the land of Egypt, from the house of bondage.*

Thou shalt fear the Lord thy God, and serve him, and shalt swear by His name.

Ye shall not go after other gods, of the gods of the people which are round about you;

(For the L<small>ORD</small> *thy God is a jealous God among you) lest the anger of the* L<small>ORD</small> *thy God be kindled against thee, and destroy thee from off the face of the earth.*

Ye shall not tempt the Lord your God, as ye tempted him in Massah.

Ye shall diligently keep the commandments of the Lord your God, and His testimonies, and His statutes, which He hath commanded thee.

And thou shalt do that which is right and good in the sight of the LORD: *that it may be well with thee, and that thou mayest go in and possess the good land which the Lord swore unto thy fathers.*

To cast out all thine enemies from before thee, as the Lord hath spoken.

And when thy son asketh thee in time to come, saying, what mean the testimonies, and the statutes, and the judgments, which the Lord our God hath commanded you?

Then thou shalt say unto thy son, we were Pharaoh's bondmen in Egypt; and the Lord brought us out of Egypt with a mighty hand:

And the Lord shewed signs and wonders, great and sore, upon Egypt, upon Pharaoh, and upon all his household, before our eyes:

And He brought us out from thence, that He might bring us in, to give us the land which He swore unto our fathers.

And the Lord commanded us to do all these statutes, to fear the Lord our God, for our good

> *always, that He might preserve us alive, as it is at this day.*
> *And it shall be our righteousness, if we observe to do all these commandments before the Lord our God, as He hath commanded us".*

Believers, our blessing is wrapped up in our obedience to God and our loyalty to His Word. Verse twelve captures God's desire for fellowship, as He tells us never to forget Him after we have eaten and become full, or in other words, whenever we are happy, satisfied, and prospering. God loves us. His desire is to have fellowship with us, and this is why He came and made His life a ransom for you and me when He died on that cross at Calvary. He died for us so that our relationship could be restored and so that we could have a chance to live and reign with Him forever. People often try to abuse the love that God has for us because they fail to recognize that, though He is a loving God, He is also a consuming fire.

> *"And it shall be, if thou do at all forget the Lord thy God, and walk after other gods, and serve them, and worship them, I testify against you this day that ye shall surely perish.*
> *As the nations which the Lord destroyeth before your face, so shall ye perish; because ye would not*

be obedient unto the voice of the Lord your God"
(Deuteronomy 8:19-20).

This is why God consistently prepares us for His blessings before elevating us. He guides us through tests and trials to reveal what resides in our hearts, observing our choices when faced with difficulty, temptation, or other challenges. Consider what emerges from you when you are under pressure. If your actions always align with the Word of God, you just need to stay steady and wait on Him. However, if you are found lacking on the test, be ready to retake it.

A trial is essentially an experiment. According to *www.thefreedictionary.com*, an experiment is 'a test under controlled conditions that is made to demonstrate a known truth, examine the validity of a hypothesis, or determine the efficacy of something previously untried.' This means that whenever we face a test, it serves to prove or confirm whether our initial plans will succeed. The outcome of any trial depends on us—our choices, reactions, and how we respond to the test.

"All the commandments which I command thee
this day shall ye observe to do, that ye may live, and
multiply, and go in and possess the land which
the Lord swore unto your fathers.
And thou shalt remember all the way which

the Lord thy God led thee these forty years in the wilderness, to humble thee, and to prove thee, to know what was in thine heart, whether thou wouldest keep His commandments, or no.

And He humbled thee, and suffered thee to hunger, and fed thee with manna, which thou knewest not, neither did thy fathers know; that He might make thee know that man doth not live by bread only, but by every word that proceedeth out of the mouth of the Lord doth man live.

Thy raiment waxed not old upon thee, neither did thy foot swell, these forty years.

Thou shalt also consider in thine heart, that, as a man chasteneth his son, so the Lord thy God chasteneth thee.

Therefore, thou shalt keep the commandments of the Lord thy God, to walk in His ways, and to fear Him.

Beware that thou forget not the Lord thy God, in not keeping His commandments, and His judgments, and His statutes, which I command thee this day: Who fed thee in the wilderness with manna, which thy fathers knew not, that He might humble thee, and that He might prove thee, to do thee good at thy latter end;

And thou say in thine heart, my power and the might of mine hand hath gotten me this wealth.

But thou shalt remember the Lord thy God: for it is He that giveth thee power to get wealth, that He may establish His covenant which He swore unto thy fathers, as it is this day" (Deuteronomy 8:1-6; 11; 16-18).

It is all about our hearts and what is in it! What could have taken the children of Israel eleven days turned into four hundred and thirty years! What a comparison! This could be you, too, but you have the power to break this vicious cycle of poverty, ignorance, rebellion, lack, you name it, by making the right choices (*more on curses in Vol. 1*).

"My son, forget not my law; but let thine heart keep my commandments:
For length of days, and long life, and peace, shall they add to thee.
Let not mercy and truth forsake thee: bind them about thy neck; write them upon the table of thine heart:
So shalt thou find favor and good understanding in the sight of God and man.
Trust in the Lord with all thine heart; and lean not unto thine own understanding.
In all thy ways acknowledge Him, and He shall direct thy paths.

Be not wise in thine own eyes: fear the Lord, and depart from evil.
It shall be health to thy navel, and marrow to thy bones" (Proverbs 3:1-8).

"If ye be willing and obedient, ye shall eat the good of the land" (Isaiah 1:19).

Second (2) Chronicles 7:14 states, *"If my people, which are called by my name, shall humble themselves and pray, and seek my face, and turn from their wicked ways; then will I hear from heaven, and will forgive their sin, and will heal their land."* God desperately wants to heal us. He wants to bless us. All we have to do is humble ourselves and realize that God is in control of our lives. We may be in charge, but God is in control; always remember that. If we repent, turn from what is wrong, and turn to Him with our whole hearts in prayer and in seeking His face, we have His promise that He will hear us. Forgiveness and deliverance are already ours; we just have to ask for them. We only need to get ourselves right with Him; what a merciful God!

Whenever someone chooses to make a spiritual change for God, be prepared! The devil and his followers will come knocking to disturb your progress in faith. A constant battle ensues. The devil recognizes a Believer's strength—although many believers are unaware of the power they hold in God. Knowing you are a threat and could become even more powerful, he will try to block your way before you reach certain spiritual levels, always trying to prevent you from advancing.

The Bible tells us in the book of Genesis that the children of Israel were more numerous than the children of Egypt, yet because of their limited way of thinking, they allowed the Egyptians to rule over them. This puzzled me. How could a great nation – mighty and great in number – allow a smaller nation to subdue them? I questioned the Lord about this, and my eyes were opened to the reality that this is still happening today as we speak. God is more powerful than the devil, and we, His children, possess the power of God. Still, we allow the devil to manipulate us and keep us in bondage while the power of God remains dormant within us. We who possess the real thing have allowed the devil to intimidate us with the power he received from God. God is in control, not the devil, and as God's children, we have an advantage over the enemy as long as we are aligned with His Word. May the Lord have mercy upon His church! Now back to what I was about to say. Remember the children of Israel when God was ready to lead them out of bondage and into their promise? As they were being led into Canaan, their land of promise, their enemies still occupied the land. God did not supernaturally kill them so they could cross over and occupy, but instead gave them the command to dispossess

THE CHOICE PATH

in order to possess. This meant war. Before they could claim their promise, they had to fight for it.

In Deuteronomy chapter seven, God told the Israelites that He would drive out their enemies before them, and they were to destroy everyone (we are always required to do our part). Even those who were in hiding would eventually be exposed. You can read part of it here.

"When the Lord thy God shall bring thee into the land whither thou goest to possess it, and hath cast out many nations before thee, the Hittites, and the Girgashites, and the Amorites, and the Canaanites, and the Perizzites, and the Hivites, and the Jebusites, seven nations greater and mightier than thou;
And when the Lord thy God shall deliver them before thee; thou shalt smite them, and utterly destroy them; thou shalt make no covenant with them, nor shew mercy unto them:" (Deuteronomy 7:1-2)

"Moreover, the Lord thy God will send the hornet among them, until they that are left, and hide themselves from thee, be destroyed.
Thou shalt not be affrighted at them: for the Lord thy God is among you, a mighty God and terrible.

> *And the Lord thy God will put out those nations before thee by little and little: thou mayest not consume them at once, lest the beasts of the field increase upon thee.*
> *But the Lord thy God shall deliver them unto thee, and shall destroy them with a mighty destruction, until they be destroyed"* (Deuteronomy 7:20-23).

Similar instructions were given to the children of Israel in Numbers 33, that they should drive out all their enemies, destroy every image and every picture, and pluck down and destroy every altar that was made to their false God.

Let me encourage you never to be afraid of change. God works in a similar way in our lives today. Each time He prepares to bless us and give us victory over a particular situation or thing, He will also bring it to the surface in our lives. God changes no one; instead, He provides the opportunity for change or an invitation to change. We must first desire change in order to change.

If anger keeps surfacing in your life, it is time to let it go. If you continually find yourself in a position where it is difficult to forgive, it is time to break down the barriers that keep you from receiving what God has for you by doing the opposite. Pay attention, and you will see what God wants to accomplish in your life.

God, in His wisdom, will never give a person more

THE CHOICE PATH

than they can handle at once. Things that need to go, which are hidden, will begin to unfold, as Deuteronomy 7:22 says, *"The Lord will drive them before you little by little that you shall not be consumed."*

What is hiding in your heart? It is time to kill everything within you that resembles the devil. Be determined and courageous to conquer and defeat every fault, bad attitude, stronghold, carnal desire, and manifestation that resides within you.

If we belong to God, we should look like Him, talk like Him, and walk like Him. He should be seen in us at all times. That is the purpose of the fire, to consume and burn out everything that is not of God within us.

Are you ready to take possession of your land? Accept His invitation to change. Destroy everything He reveals to you that is of the devil by refusing to act, speak, and partake of evil. Live according to His ways and watch what God will do for you. Aim for the sky and shoot for the stars because you can go as far as you are willing to go with God.

> *"According as His divine power hath given unto us all things that pertain unto life and godliness, through the knowledge of Him that hath called us to glory and virtue"* (2 Peter 1:3).

This is how Christ is revealed to His people and to the world. May God have His way in our lives so that His power may return to the churches through us, His people; Amen.

> *"He that hath my commandments, and keepeth them, he it is that loveth me: and he that loveth me shall be loved of my Father, and I will love him, and will manifest myself to him.*
> *Judas saith unto Him, not Iscariot, Lord, how is it that thou wilt manifest thyself unto us, and not unto the world?*
> *Jesus answered and said unto him, if a man loves me, he will keep my words: and my Father will love him, and we will come unto him, and make our abode with him"* (St. John 14: 21-23).

Other Scripture References:

2 Chronicles 6
2 Chronicles 7

TIMELY THOUGHTS

- Your success in life is not determined by God but by your obedience to Him.
- How much of God you will acquire (power) is not determined by Him but by your daily living, which spells sacrifice and CHOICE.
- The devil is not your greatest enemy. YOU are.
- God has already given us everything we need for life and godliness.
- Your breakthrough is within you.

8
FOUR PRINCIPLES FOR SUCCESS

God has already given us His blueprint, and there is no way around it. The choice is ours to accept if we desire to be blessed by God; it is not entirely left up to Him. If we accept God's Word and remain obedient to Him, we will be blessed. If we disobey His Word and live according to the imagination of our hearts, we will be cursed and ultimately destroyed. If we choose to honor God, we will be rewarded. If we choose to dishonor God, we will be rewarded accordingly.

Our choices have consequences, whether good or bad, and, at the end of the day, they will determine our outcome. It's your choice! This is why it is important for us to allow the Word of God to rule our hearts daily. King David said in the book of Psalms, *"Thy words have I hid in my heart that I may not sin against thee."*

The Word of God acts as a shield for us, but it will be of no effect in our lives if we fail to understand it. Do you remember the parable of the sower and the seeds in St. Matthew 13? Seeds sown in different grounds produced different results, and the seeds that brought forth fruit were those sown in good soil. The seeds represent the Word of God, and the ground represents our hearts. If God's Word is not hidden in our hearts daily, we will not be able to remember His Word in times of need, as the parable of St. Matthew 13 suggests. These are the times when we need it most.

For the Word of God to be truly effective in our lives, every child of God should make a habit of meditating on God's Word each day. Daily meditation fosters understanding, which leads to spiritual growth, and eventually, strong roots are established.

When you reach a stage in your relationship with God where His Word is always on your mind, and you make decisions based on it, your heart is governed by His Word. This makes it much easier to face challenges, as the Word is ready in your heart to guide and instruct you on how to respond appropriately as a child of God.

Like the Apostle Paul, I encourage you to allow the Word of God to dwell richly in your heart; keep it alive there always. This will ensure more victories in your life. All God wants is a man or a woman who will give Him their heart entirely. He wants a relationship that is out of

FOUR PRINCIPLES FOR SUCCESS

the ordinary so that He can be a God to His people and His people can have Him as their God.

God desires closeness, and closeness comes only through obedience and loyalty to God's Word, no matter what.

> *"These evil people, who refuse to hear my words, who walk in the imagination of their heart, and walk after other gods, to serve them, and to worship them, shall even be as this girdle, which is good for nothing.*
> *For as the girdle cleaveth to the loins of a man, so have I caused to cleave unto me the whole house of Israel and the whole house of Judah, saith the LORD; that they might be unto me for a people, and for a name, and for a praise, and for a glory: but they would not hear" (Jeremiah 13:10-11).*

> *"But this thing commanded I them, saying, obey my voice, and I will be your God, and ye shall be my people: and walk ye in all the ways that I have commanded you, that it may be well unto you. But they hearkened not, nor inclined their ear, but walked in the counsels and in the imagination of their evil heart, and went backward, and not forward" (Jeremiah 7:23-24).*

> "He that overcometh shall inherit all things; and I will be his God, and he shall be my son" (Revelation 21:7).

Principle #1: Identify the strongman governing your life

Our natural state reflects our spiritual state, so whatever occurs in the spiritual realm regarding our lives will affect us in the physical realm as well. Remember the woman with the spirit of infirmity for eighteen years? She was bound spiritually, and this affected her natural state, as her physical body appeared deformed.

The Bible tells us the cause of her situation. The devil had her bound for eighteen years, but praise God, He stepped in. Her problem was addressed from a spiritual perspective. Jesus identified the binding on her life, then He loosed her, and she was made whole as she was set free. You can read the story in St. Luke chapter thirteen when you get the chance. God already knows every person who belongs to Him, and we can rest assured that He is with us. He has given us His angels for protection, and these angels are commonly called guardian angels. Before we can talk about success, we need to realize that just as we have angels assigned to us for protection, so too demons are assigned to us to block and ultimately hinder the purposes of God from coming to pass in our lives.

Every person has a demonic spirit assigned to his or her life to derail them, stunt growth, and eventually abort the will of God for their lives. These spirits on assignment are responsible for nurturing and instilling us with the wrong beliefs. If we carefully roll back the curtain of memories, I am certain you will see how these spirits have managed to sow evil seeds within us, one way or another. It is also my belief that demonic spirits are assigned to individuals based on the purpose or the mantle that rests heavily upon that individual.

This is why it is important to understand that before anyone can experience success in their lives, they must first identify the strong man ruling their lives and conquer him. Battles will be fewer, and victories will become easier for the individual who learns how to identify the strongman governing his/her life and consistently wage war against that spirit in prayer and by becoming practical.

The process of identifying the strongman set over our lives should be guided by intense prayer, spiritual reflection, and spiritual discernment. Along with that, ask yourself these questions: What bothers me most, or what am I constantly affected by? Do I walk around with grave concerns about what others think of me (fear is an underlying factor)? Or do I care a great deal about my self-image – how I am seen in the eyes of others (leviathan – the spirit of pride)? Do I always have to be right, or do I feel the need to control everyone and everything around me (another manifestation of pride, or could it stem from fear)?

Ask yourself those questions, then prayerfully meditate and ask God to reveal to you the hidden things in your heart and to give you the discernment to understand them. Compare what bothers you most with your past and identify the root of your actions. Based on the knowledge I have, I believe the devil primarily manipulates people through two main spirits: the spirit of Leviathan, which represents pride, and the spirit of the dragon, symbolizing fear. I am confident that many, if not all, problems can often be traced back to these two spirits — either pride or fear.

If you closely analyze what I am saying, you'll find the connection. These spirits work alongside others, often called underlings or footmen, to destroy people's lives. However, by peeling back the layers, you'll generally find that fear or pride is involved, as they are usually the masterminds behind most problems. The Bible also mentions the spirit of behemoth, which is compared to the chief ways of God. I have never asked the Lord about this spirit before, so always seek divine guidance, as there is always more to learn. At this stage, you may not yet be able to identify the main spirit behind your problem, but once you do, you will be well on your way. Take it before the Lord daily in prayer, and He will speak. You can also seek counsel in this area from a good steward of the Word, such as your pastor if he or she is a sound student of the Word, but give yourself time to develop and become mature in God.

> *"Or else how can one enter into a strong man's house, and spoil his goods, except he first bind the strong man? And then he will spoil his house"*
> *(Matthew 12:29).*

Many Christians do not understand this principle, and as a result, they pray incorrectly and see little or no results. There is a right way to warfare. Many people pray against demonic spirits randomly, but the correct way is to first identify the ruling spirit, or strongman, over your life, community, business, etc., and pray against that spirit; the underlings under the ruling spirit's control will be rendered ineffective once the strongman loses its power.

In my experience, the spirit of the dragon was the dominant force in my life—and it continues to influence many lives as you're reading. This spirit manipulates its victims through fear, which I struggled with for many years. It felt like fear was constantly present, always ready to seize the moment and take hold of me. Out of this fear, I constructed a personal world based on the lies that the devil had sown in my heart.

I grew up feeling unloved and rejected, and it all stemmed from fear. I walked daily in a world that never existed, one that was only imaginary, because my eyes were clouded by the truth, and I conformed to the lies the devil showed me from the pit of hell (*I spoke exclusively about this in Book 1 – "The Revelation of the Dragon: No More Walls"; please see for a detailed discussion*).

I remember losing my father at an early age. After I got married, I lost my first child, a baby girl, hours after giving birth due to hospital negligence, and I felt like I had lost everything. This was one of the most devastating times in my life, and the devil saw it as a perfect opportunity and capitalized on it. It was then that the spirit of fear made a deeper move into my life, and I suffered from great fear thereafter. I thought everyone around me was going to die! I began to lose hope, and my struggle with fear intensified immensely because of the trauma. I became stressed, but fear had no mercy because it brought anxiety and mild depression along with it.

I was not only fearful of losing my loved ones, but I also became fearful in many ways, and this was when I realized that fear was present with me. I was fearful of taking risks and of putting myself on the line, especially when it came to love and happiness. I feared that the moment I let go and became happy, my happiness would be taken from me, so I decided to remain unhappy,

FOUR PRINCIPLES FOR SUCCESS

believing that happiness was something I would eventually lose – or so I thought.

My reasoning was flawed, and I was unwilling to risk becoming happy only to later lose this coveted emotion. So I decided to remain unhappy in an effort to protect myself from unnecessary suffering, not realizing that I was already suffering unnecessarily by choosing to deny myself happiness.

This went on for years, and it was not until I encountered God that things began to change. For many years, I prayed against the spirits of poverty, lack, and fear, and nothing much happened. There were times when my family received raindrops, but there was no rain – no outpouring – until we turned to God fully. After the Lord revealed the main culprit behind our problems, He gave me a strategy to pray against this spirit, and things have never been the same since (*I spoke about this in detail in "The Revelation of the Dragon: No More Walls Bk. 1"*).

What we tried to change on our own for years suddenly changed without us even trying! That was when the Lord spoke to me about fighting the wrong way. We tend to pray our way up – listing every spirit we believe is affecting our lives, never reaching the head of the list – when we were meant to pray our way down. If we strike the head, the body will fall, and if we kill the spider, there will be no more spider webs – are you following me? The web is not the problem; the spider is, so do not waste your precious time tearing down spider webs while the spider remains loose; get the spider first, and you will get rid of the cobwebs.

This is why we need to turn to God with all of our hearts if we desire success. Had we not turned to God with our entire hearts, I can guarantee you that we would still be stuck in the same position, praying blindly for change. Knowledge comes from God, and if we are going to be successful, we must turn to God so that He can reveal what is happening in our lives and show us how to deal with it. We must become totally dependent on God for knowledge!

When you live for God the way He wants you to and give your entire heart to Him, there is no doubt that God will watch over and protect you. God will not sit back and watch your enemies triumph over you; He will intervene and expose the devil's plans for your life as it pleases Him.

If you do not understand what is taking place in your life, just live holy for God. If you want to experience victory or change, just remain obedient to God and His Word. If you want to see God move on your behalf, just stay in the fire when you are being tested. God will eventually show up once you stand for Him. When you go all out for God, curses will be broken, and deliverance will follow without you even trying to accomplish it. Success will be sure and evident. That is the power of having God's presence and acknowledging Him in everything you do.

FOUR PRINCIPLES FOR SUCCESS

As you remain open and pure before God, honoring Him by being obedient to His Word, God will reveal to you strategies and the knowledge needed for added power. God will honor you, exalt you, and make you, in return, a ruler in His Kingdom. How would you like that! He will promote you and establish you so that people will be astonished when they look at you. He will make you a judge and a security officer for His Kingdom, but the price is to walk in His ways by being obedient. Are you willing? Stay in your fire and allow God to process you, because you will be branded. This brand or mark that will be placed on you is very visible in the realm of the spirit and will also act as a covering for you. Your protection is right there; stay in your fire, and God will take you out once your process is complete. Here it is, right here.

> *"And he shewed me Joshua the high priest standing before the angel of the LORD, and Satan standing at his right hand to resist him.*
> *And the LORD said unto Satan, The LORD rebuke thee, O Satan; even the LORD that hath chosen Jerusalem rebuke thee: is not this a brand plucked out of the fire?*
> *Now Joshua was clothed with filthy garments and stood before the angel.*
> *And he answered and spake unto those that stood before him, saying, Take away the filthy garments*

from him. And unto him he said, Behold, I have caused thine iniquity to pass from thee, and I will clothe thee with change of raiment.

And I said, let them set a fair mitre upon his head. So, they set a fair mitre upon his head and clothed him with garments. And the angel of the LORD stood by.

And the angel of the LORD protested unto Joshua, saying,

Thus saith the LORD of hosts: If thou wilt walk in my ways, and if thou wilt keep my charge, then thou shalt also judge my house, and shalt also keep my courts, and I will give thee places to walk among these that stand by.

Hear now, O Joshua the high priest, thou, and thy fellows that sit before thee: for they are men wondered at: for, behold, I will bring forth my servant the BRANCH.

For behold the stone that I have laid before Joshua; upon one stone shall be seven eyes: behold, I will engrave the graving thereof, saith the LORD of hosts, and I will remove the iniquity of that land in one day.

In that day, saith the LORD of hosts, shall ye call every man his neighbor under the vine and under the fig tree" (Zechariah 3: 1-10).

FOUR PRINCIPLES FOR SUCCESS

If you are struggling with fear, dryness, lack, barrenness, confusion, missed opportunities, lack of productivity or growth, failure, discouragement, disappointment, suppression, or oppression, etc., the spirit of the dragon is the mastermind behind your problems.

The spirit of the dragon uses fear to produce unfruitfulness and everything mentioned above (*see also "The Revelation of the Dragon," Bk. 1, for more information*). If this cycle is to be broken, we must align with God's principles and the laws He has established that govern the universe. Once we come into agreement with these principles, we will become prosperous without doubt.

Principle #2: Walk within your assignment – your God-given purpose

When you step into the divine purpose that God has established for you, you will have God on your side. When you come into agreement with what God has called you to do and begin to flow in it, you will have the laws of the universe to assist you. It is similar to the law of the seed. Outside of soil, without water, and without sunlight, a seed loses its power and will not grow; once placed in soil, watered, and exposed to sunlight, it will grow successfully. This is because there are laws that govern the germination of seeds, and the same principle applies to you and me. Once we discover our God-given purpose and move along that path, our lives will change significantly because that is how God has designed it.

I am not saying that things will always go smoothly as planned, because there will always be obstacles in our way. The devil knows that when we walk in our God-given assignment, we will become unstoppable, and he is afraid of this, hence the fights; but God will always make things happen for us if we remain faithful and continue to step out in faith on His Word.

You will never become the best you can be until you begin to embrace your purpose. It is a powerful thing to walk in your God-given assignment. For your obedience and persistence, God will bless and prosper you. God will work things out for you in ways you never imagined. Wouldn't that be better than embracing your own will and your own desires? Doing that would be like planting a seed in stony ground and then working hard to oversee its growth in the wrong soil. That situation would require more time, energy, and effort to cultivate and nurture that seed into life, if possible.

It is difficult to make your own plans work in place of God's will. If you desire to be successful in any way, you need to come into agreement with God by accepting His plans for your life in every way possible.

The law of attraction is very powerful. It is a set of systematic actions that are triggered by our own actions.

FOUR PRINCIPLES FOR SUCCESS

We must be careful to do the right thing so that the desired results may be triggered or produced. When we come into agreement with God, His laws will align with us, and the universe will respond. Time will yield the results.

Principle #3 – The law of attraction

The universe is governed by laws established by principles. The Word of God tells us that there is no respect of persons with God, and I am beginning to understand this more and more each day.

Based on the principles of God that have been established, I find that you could be a man of faith or a woman of prayer and remain the same, except that you come into and abide by the laws of God, which are governed by His Word. So, though you may pray day and night for a miracle or fast often for your breakthrough, God cannot and will not answer your prayers until you come into alignment with His principles. Let's take another look at Romans 13:1-4 to gain a better understanding.

> *"Let every soul be subject unto the higher powers. For there is no power but of God: the powers that be are ordained of God.*
> *Whosoever therefore resisteth the power, resisteth the ordinance of God: and they that resist shall receive to themselves damnation.*

> *For rulers are not a terror to good works, but to the evil. Wilt thou then not be afraid of the power? Do that which is good, and thou shalt have praise of the same:*
> *For he is the minister of God to thee for good. But if thou do that which is evil, be afraid; for he beareth not the sword in vain: for he is the minister of God, a revenger to execute wrath upon him that doeth evil".*

It doesn't matter who you are, your anointing, your power in God, or the secrets God has revealed to you; stepping beyond your boundaries or violating God's principles will lead to consequences outside of God's control. God's laws are firm—He has already spoken His Word, which will not return empty but will achieve its purpose. I see clearly why Hosea says, *"My people are destroyed for lack of knowledge."*

> *"So shall my word be that goeth forth out of my mouth: it shall not return unto me void, but it shall accomplish that which I please, and it shall prosper in the thing whereto I sent it"* (Isaiah 55:11).

This is one reason some Believers have been praying for years yet still need a breakthrough. There are Believers who tithe yet still struggle to afford a meal, even though Malachi 3 says, *"Bring ye all the tithes into the storehouse, that there may be meat in mine house, and prove me now herewith, saith the LORD of hosts, if I will not open you the windows of heaven, and pour you out a blessing, that there shall not be room enough to receive it.*

And I will rebuke the devourer for your sake, and he shall not destroy the fruits of your ground; neither shall your vine cast her fruit before the time in the field, saith the LORD of hosts."

God honors His Word above His name, and if we do not align ourselves with the principles God has established, we will not experience His undiluted power or favor in our lives.

James chapter 2 tells us that if we obey the whole law and offend in one point, we are guilty of all. This is something worthy of meditation. It is our responsibility to ensure that every area of our lives is in accordance with God's standards so that we can experience His fullness.

The Bible also tells us that *if iniquity is in our hearts, God will not hear us.* It is pointless to pray and ask God to forgive us, lay out our petitions before Him, and return to our old ways while claiming the promises of God if we are not willing to change.

"If my people, who are called by my name, shall humble themselves, and pray, and seek my face, and

> *turn from their wicked ways; then will I hear from heaven, and will forgive their sin, and will heal their land"* (2 Chronicles 7:14).

Please note the part that says turn. If we repent and change our evil ways, God is merciful enough to heal our lives, but we must first be willing to change course.

Many Believers mistakenly hold onto God's promises while living in contradiction to His Word. Some believe these promises are guaranteed simply because they call themselves "Christian," but receiving God's ultimate blessings requires obedience and dedication to His Word.

Jesus asked in Luke 6, *"Why call ye me Lord, Lord, and do not the things that I say?"* We must become doers of the Word and not hearers only, as James instructs. In a previous chapter, I explained the law governing the formation of water into ice. The water must be exposed to temperatures at the freezing point and remain there for a period of time before it can be transformed.

Can you get ice cubes by placing an ice tray filled with water into a fridge? The answer is no. You could leave it in the fridge and pray for years, but the water will not turn into ice until it is placed at the correct temperature (the freezer) and left there long enough. The temperature conditions must be right before water can be turned into ice, and so it is with our relationship with God (see Keys to the Kingdom: Unlocking the Mystery of Prayer for more).

FOUR PRINCIPLES FOR SUCCESS

We must live up to God's standards and meet His requirements as explained in His Word before we can reap success in abundance.

There are so many Christians who use the Word of God out of context, frustrating themselves and becoming discouraged, expecting God to work on their behalf when God can do nothing outside His principles. This is the process God has established, and if we desire success, we need to come into agreement with His laws and strive to live up to His standards in order to see God at work in our lives in an amazing way that will blow our minds and leave us in awe.

Cultivate the life you desire by practicing to live by the principle that governs the law of attraction, God's way. The Word of God says: give and it shall be given; treat others as you desire to be treated; whatever you sow is what you will reap; if you sow to the flesh, you will reap corruption of the flesh, but if you sow to the spirit, you will reap life of the spirit. The Bible goes further to tell us: if we sow sparingly, we will reap sparingly, but if we sow abundantly, we will reap abundantly; cast your bread upon the waters and you will find it after many days; judge not and you will not be judged; condemn not and you will not be condemned; forgive and you will be forgiven; and so much more. These are all laws of attraction; like attracts like.

Whatever you practice or whatever seed you sow in

this life, that seed will be measured back to you. Again, this is why the Bible encourages us to: love our enemies; do good to those who hate us; bless those who curse us; and pray for those who spitefully use us. It is a requirement to love and not hate, and to bless and not curse, because whatever we do will be measured back to us, and that will be our reward in the end – that which we attract to ourselves. Live by the golden rule; treat people as you would like to be treated, because payday is certain, and our reward is determined by our deeds.

> *"But I say unto you, which hear, love your enemies, do good to them which hate you,*
> *Bless them that curse you, and pray for them which despitefully use you.*
> *And unto him that smiteth thee on the one cheek offer also the other; and him that taketh away thy cloke forbid not to take thy coat also.*
> *Give to every man that asketh of thee; and of him that taketh away thy goods ask them not again.*
> *And as ye would that men should do to you, do ye also to them likewise.*
> *For if ye love them which love you, what thank have ye? For sinners also love those who love them.*
> *And if ye do good to them which do good to you, what thank have ye? For sinners also do even the same.*

And if ye lend to them of whom ye hope to receive, what thank have ye? For sinners also lend to sinners, to receive as much again.

But love ye your enemies, and do good, and lend, hoping for nothing again; and your reward shall be great, and ye shall be the children of the Highest: for He is kind unto the unthankful and to the evil.

Be ye therefore merciful, as your Father also is merciful.

Judge not, and ye shall not be judged: condemn not, and ye shall not be condemned: forgive, and ye shall be forgiven:

Give, and it shall be given unto you; good measure, pressed down, and shaken together, and running over, shall men give into your bosom. For with the same measure that ye mete withal it shall be measured to you again" (Luke 6:27-38).

"Now therefore, if ye will obey my voice indeed, and keep my covenant, then ye shall be a peculiar treasure unto me above all people: for all the earth is mine:

And ye shall be unto me a Kingdom of priests, and a holy nation. These are the words which thou shalt speak unto the children of Israel" (Exodus 19:5).

Principle# 4 - Timing

Every seed has an incubation period, including those sown as good deeds in individuals' lives. This is another of God's laws; the principle of timing. Timing is everything. After we have done what God requires of us, we must be willing to actively wait with patience for the promise.

When you put water into an ice tray and place it in the freezer to make ice cubes, you cannot go back in 5 minutes or even an hour later and expect to get well-formed cubes. You need to wait for a period before the cubes are fully formed, and this period depends on two factors: the temperature and the size of the cubes you intend to produce. The smaller the size, the faster the results, and the colder the temperature, the less time you will have to wait. Another factor that will affect this transformation process is impurities.

You cannot remain obedient to God's Word and not be blessed. It is impossible because God's Word does not lie. The Bible tells us that *"Obedience is better than sacrifice,"* and that's all that God desires from us, our obedience.

After you have done your part, practice the seven processes discussed in this book and wait. There is a time and a season for everything under the sun. There is a time set for us to endure what we must, and we only need to be willing to complete our process to the end without compromise, but with commitment and consistency. I urge you, however, not to get caught in the deceptive web of waiting patiently on God without first doing what is required of you. Before we can get to the waiting part of the process, we must DO our part; then, and only then, will we be qualified to wait. I caution you also not to be deceived into waiting while doing nothing. Faith without works is dead, and in order for God to do His part, something will be required from you as well.

Believers, I implore you; be alert, stay in your process, and wait patiently on God. When God says move, go, even when you cannot see your way clearly. Just trust Him and do not let God's timing pass you by, because no one knows when their next season will come. Missing your season would lengthen your process and delay God's plan for your life, as it did for the children of Israel. So, I encourage you to wait on God, but move with His timing.

Will you give Him ALL of your heart today? Will you trust Him? Are you ready to say yes to Him? Then say this prayer with me.

Prayer

Father, I thank you for your love, for while I was yet a sinner, you died for me. What would I do without your love, Lord? Thank you for your mercy. Forgive me of all my sins, purify my heart, and remove all my fears, doubts, and worries, in Jesus' name.

Father, I pray that you will remove the pain of my past from my spirit and cleanse me with your blood. Deliver me from every hurt and from those who seek to control my life. Give me the strength and grace I need to endure. I invite you now to come into my heart and take over my life. I ask that you help me honor you in all I do and say. Help me prove my love for you by being faithful and obedient to your Word. May my ways be pleasing to you always, and may your strength be made perfect in my times of weakness. Father, I give it all to you now; help me along the way and make me whole as I make this conscious decision to serve you better. In Jesus' name I pray; Amen.

If you just prayed this prayer, all you have to do is believe. Believe that God is with you and that He will order and direct your steps once you acknowledge Him. God is with you every step of the way, and He will be with you to the end as long as you stay on the path He has placed you on. He has given us His Word as a guide. Follow His instructions, and you will see the reward.

There are seasons and a time for everything. We must be willing to wait upon God to mature the seed we have deposited (*Paul planted, Apollos watered, but God gives the increase - 1 Corinthians 3:6*), so I say again, wait upon the Lord.

Turn to God with your whole heart and be obedient to Him when He speaks. Identify and break the power of the strong man governing your life, say yes to your God-given purpose, come into agreement with God and abide by His principles, travel on the roads to success discussed in this book, and stay on the paths mentioned. I guarantee you that God's Word guarantees you success.

"And so, after he had patiently endured, he obtained the promise" (Hebrews 6:15).

The Seven Processes

1. The Process of the Heart
2. The Process of Relationship
3. The Process of Purification
4. The Process of Freedom
5. The Process of Determination
6. The Process of Confidence
7. The Process of Choice

Four Principles for Success

1. Identify and destroy the strongman who governs your life
2. Walk within your God-given purpose/assignment
3. Acknowledge and enforce God's law of attraction
4. Timing – wait for it after you have done your part

FOUR PRINCIPLES FOR SUCCESS

"And let us not be weary in well doing: for in due season we shall reap, if we faint not" (Galatians 6:9).

ABOUT THE AUTHOR

Change your thoughts, change your world; transform your future.

Your mind is powerful. It can affect lives through a recognized, established pattern of thinking, and Terryann is on a mission to transform lives by transforming minds through the Word of God. Minister Scott is the author of the powerful, life-changing series entitled "No More," among other works. Her writings are steered towards spiritual warfare, personal development, inner healing, and spiritual upliftment, providing *"Empowerment for the Total You."* Her writings have impacted many and are tried, true, and inspired by the Holy Spirit.

Mrs. Scott is also an Educator, Speaker, Publisher, and Workshop Facilitator, among other things. She carries the mandate of helping married couples and also those who are abused and broken. Her ministry seeks to help persons to "identify their purpose and walk into their God-given destiny." She is passionate about spreading the undiluted Gospel across the globe, and watching the power of God return in the church to restore broken lives through Healing and Deliverance is just a part of her vision.

Minister Scott believes knowledge is power, and, in alignment with this, her mission is to educate, motivate, encourage, and foster growth through workshops and other coaching sessions.

Terryann's voice is instituted to nurture and restore the body of Christ by revealing hidden truths while exploring matters of the heart that will enable the end-time army of God to regain her actual shape and form in Christ. She is very passionate about transforming lives and fulfilling her call according to Isaiah 61: 1-4; which is to "Heal the brokenhearted, set the oppressed free, comfort those who mourn, and to deliver those who are bound by the proclamation of the Gospel of Jesus Christ, in Spirit and power through the working of the Holy Spirit." Her messages can be heard internationally on the airwaves in some parts of the USA and the Caribbean.

Minister Scott has appeared in several magazines and has contributed to two published works in addition to her own.

Terryann is married to Praise and Worship Leader, Danever Scott, who is also a Minister of Religion, Producer, and Sound Engineer, among other things. The couple has three beautiful children together – Danaevia, Judah, and Kayla Scott, of whom the first is deceased. Through much heartache and pain, the couple has attained a closer walk with God, and they continue to share their story, offering hope to many.

LET'S CONNECT

------

*Do you have a Supernatural Encounter you would like to share? Submit your stories to **info.scottspublishing@gmail.com** along with your full name, location, and occupation. Submissions will be collated and published as an eBook. Your experience matters and may be what someone needs to hear.*

------

*Connect with me on **Facebook** (don't forget to like my page) and on other social media sites such as **X, YouTube,** and **Instagram.***

May God bless you, and I do look forward to connecting.

LET'S CONNECT

For updates and new releases, follow me on Amazon.

Please submit a review for this devotional HERE. Your reviews are essential and will help others to find this free devotional guide. Your reviews will also help spread the message of the Gospel and inner healing to others across the globe. Tell your family and friends about this free devotional and invite them to download it. This guide may be precisely what they need during difficult times.

Check out my other titles.

BOOKS BY TERRYANN SCOTT

Please visit Amazon to see a complete list

The Revelation of the Dragon: No More Walls - Vol. 1 of "The 'No More' Series"

MY ENTIRE LIFE CHANGED, AND YOURS

BOOKS BY TERRYANN SCOTT

CAN TOO by simply utilizing this powerful warfare strategy that God has released for His people.

"The Revelation of the Dragon: No More Walls" exposes the forces of darkness behind the longstanding cycles of disappointment, setbacks, fear, confusion, lack, poverty, and so much more.

This revelation came at the most trying and difficult time of my life, and it led me on a journey of self-discovery and a search for God. After my husband and I radically sought God, God stepped in, delivered our family, and revealed the culprit that was behind our struggles. I recognized almost immediately that a terribly longstanding cycle of pain, misery, and carry-overs was broken from our lives with very little effort on our part, except by being obedient to God and through maintaining a closer walk with Him.

BOOKS BY TERRYANN SCOTT

Roads to Success: No More Barriers - Vol. 2 of "The 'No More' Series"

Every person has a strong man governing their life, and to be successful, that strong man must first be identified and defeated. In Volume 1, *The Revelation of the Dragon: No More Walls*, Terryann Scott exposes a powerful spirit behind long-standing struggles such as disappointments, dryness, and lack in people's lives.

In Volume 2, *Roads to Success: No More Barriers*, Minister Scott reveals two hidden paths and five main roads you'll want to travel on for guaranteed success.

Mrs. Scott unfolds the heart of God towards His people while exposing seven Biblical Processes and four Biblical Principles that will transform your life from barrenness to fruitfulness.

In this book, you will:

- Learn the seven Biblical Processes and four Biblical Principles for guaranteed success.
- Discover how your past may be holding you back.
- Identify hidden blocks from your past and learn how to overcome them.
- Discover the heart of God, His promises towards His children, and how to acquire them.
- Discover the role of your obedience to God.
- Identify 'roads' to travel on daily for guaranteed success and
- Learn how you can use the law of attraction by God's design to create the life you've always dreamed of, God's way.

Do not stop here, a new life awaits you! I know you will be blessed.

"Your success in life is not determined by God, but by your obedience to Him."
~ Terryann Scott.

BOOKS BY TERRYANN SCOTT

Keys to the Kingdom: Unlocking the Mysteries of Prayer

Why are some prayers answered and not others? Why does a good God allow bad things to happen to people? Why am I praying, but I'm not getting my prayers answered? Is God real? If you are curious about the Mysteries of the Kingdom and how to get your prayers answered, then this book is for you.

In this book, Minister Terryann Scott shares personal stories and testimonies from spiritual encounters with Jesus and supernatural revelations received in the spiritual realm.

Just as there are laws that govern the formation of water into ice, so too there are spiritual laws that govern prayer. If these laws are not understood and if the conditions required for prayer are not met, our prayers will not be answered.

BOOKS BY TERRYANN SCOTT

I am so excited to share with you what the Lord has taught me about prayer and Kingdom power. Join me now for this intense read as we take a peek into the supernatural realm to discover how to get your prayers answered and unlock the Mystery of Prayer.

BOOKS BY TERRYANN SCOTT

Becoming a Better You: Heal Your Soul; Heal Your Life

Unhealthy patterns and cycles are the result of a wounded soul that needs to be healed. Life's challenges can leave us beaten and worn, and the anxiety, worry, stress, and other adverse effects associated with the struggles we endure can prevent us from shining like the person we were created to be. A toxic mind will lead to a toxic life, and if you desire a healthy life, you have to acquire a healthy mind and a free spirit. Discover how to get healed from the soul level and give birth to your God-given destiny by using this three-step strategy that God has given me.

A new life awaits you. It's time to become a better you! Let's go!

BOOKS BY TERRYANN SCOTT

Surviving Challenging Times: Faith Devotional

Why does God allow hardship? Where is He when life feels overwhelming? Does He truly care?

These are the questions many believers wrestle with during seasons of pain, loss, uncertainty, and waiting. When challenges arise, it can be difficult to think clearly or hold onto hope—especially when fear, anxiety, and discouragement begin to take root.

Surviving Challenging Times was created for those moments.

This 21-week devotional is designed to strengthen your faith, renew your mind, and uplift your spirit when life feels heavy. Through weekly reflections grounded in Scripture and faith-filled encouragement, this devotional gently guides you to see beyond your circumstances and rediscover God's presence, love, and purpose—even in the midst of difficulty.

Rather than merely helping you endure, *Surviving Challenging Times* challenges you to grow. It inspires a new way of thinking rooted in trust, hope, and spiritual resilience, so you can move from merely surviving to experiencing the blessings of steadfast faith.

If you are feeling drained, burdened, discouraged, or uncertain about the future, this devotional will help you refocus your heart on God's truth and promises.

Are you ready to strengthen your faith and rise above life's challenges?

Join this 21-week journey of reflection, renewal, and spiritual growth—and discover how faith can carry you through even the most challenging seasons.

BOOKS BY TERRYANN SCOTT

Overcoming Obstacles: Hope Devotional
eBook available FREE on popular retailer sites

Are you struggling with inner fears, emotional wounds, or the desire to give up?

Forgiving those who have caused deep pain—and finding the confidence to move forward after broken relationships—can feel overwhelming. Lingering memories, damaged self-worth, and unhealed emotions often keep us stuck. Yet healing is possible with guidance, faith, and a renewed way of thinking.

Overcoming Obstacles is an inner-healing devotional guide designed to help you heal your heart, renew your mind, and rediscover your God-given purpose. Every person was designed with intention, but before purpose can be fully revealed and fulfilled, the heart must be restored, and the mind transformed.

This devotional is written for those facing emotional

and mental challenges, especially believers who struggle with fear, self-image, confidence, and self-worth. Through faith-centered reflections and practical spiritual insights, it offers hope and encouragement while guiding you toward lasting inner healing.

Overcoming Obstacles includes fourteen devotionals that can be used daily or weekly as a foundational guide. While not a comprehensive manual on inner healing, it shares personal insights that help Christian believers discover their identity in God, shift their perspective, and grow emotionally and spiritually.

This is an invitation to reflect, heal, and move forward with faith.

Are you ready to confront what's holding you back and begin the journey toward wholeness?

BOOKS BY TERRYANN SCOTT

Hidden Truths: Daily Devotional

Hidden Truths is a powerful daily devotional that equips Christian believers with spiritual wisdom, biblical discernment, and eye-opening insights rooted in God's Word. In a world where deception often disguises itself as light, this devotional helps expose the subtle and hidden works of the enemy while pointing readers back to the unchanging truth of Scripture.

Discernment is a vital part of the believer's walk with Christ. The Bible warns that not everything that appears good is truly from God, and that even the devil can present himself as an angel of light. Hidden Truths encourages readers to test every spirit, grow in spiritual awareness, and guard their hearts against deception through prayer, reflection, and biblical truth.

Each devotional is thoughtfully written to be educational, thought-provoking, and spiritually awakening, stirring the believer's heart toward a deeper, more intimate relationship with God. While not exhaustive, this devotional offers personal insights and practical spiritual reflections to help Christians grow in knowledge, faith, and spiritual maturity.

Perfect for daily reading, Hidden Truths invites readers to pause, meditate, and pray after each entry—creating space to hear God more clearly, strengthen discernment, and discover Him in a fresh and meaningful way.

Ideal for:

- Christians seeking spiritual growth
- Believers desiring deeper discernment
- Daily devotional and prayer time
- Personal reflection or small group study

BOOKS BY TERRYANN SCOTT

Finding God: Love Devotional

Finding God is about pursuing Him. It is about going after God with all your heart and discovering Him, especially in hard times. God is almost always discovered through pain, based on the individual's response to the challenge, and pain can therefore be a blessing in disguise when used to draw near to God.

I discovered God through much heartache and pain (I spoke about this in *The Revelation of the Dragon: No More Walls, vol. 1*). *I remember when I thought my life was over and that* the only person I had left was God. This caused me to experience a rude awakening, which brought me closer to Him. I was a Christian for many years, but it was not until I found Him in such a profound way that I realized I was like Peter, walking with God, but not converted.

After my conversion, I noticed that things changed

dramatically with only a little prayer and sincere effort on my part, as I focused on God and put His Word into practice. I was amazed at how much I discovered God, so much so that I decided to marry my newfound lifestyle with much prayer. That was when I found it is not just in the praying, but in the doing. There are many men and women of prayer whose lives remain the same because they are hearers of the Word and not doers.

My eyes were immediately opened as I discovered the seriousness of living out the Word of God in obedience and merging that lifestyle with prayer. I got astounding results with little prayer and by becoming a doer of the Word, rather than just a hearer, compared to much prayer and no results due to a lack of practicality. What we do is more important to God than what we pray and how long we pray. God honors our lifestyle and obedience above our prayers.

God is a practical God, and if you need results, follow me for a few days on this journey throughout our Love devotional guide. Are you ready to discover His presence?

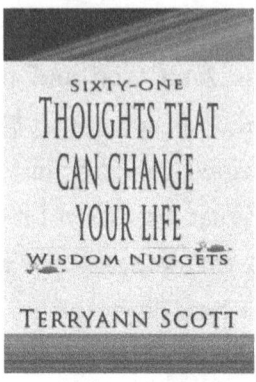

Sixty-One Thoughts That Can Change Your Life: Wisdom Nuggets

One thought can shift your perspective. Sixty-one can transform your life.

This book is a personal compilation of **sixty-one powerful spiritual thoughts** drawn from deep reflection, prayer, and meditation on the Word of God. Each thought is designed to inspire clarity, strengthen faith, and invite meaningful change through intentional application in everyday life.

These reflections are not theoretical—they are practical, faith-centered insights meant to be lived. When embraced and applied, they encourage spiritual growth, renewed thinking, and a deeper connection with God.

Whether read slowly for reflection or revisited during moments of prayer and study, these spiritual thoughts serve as gentle reminders of God's truth, purpose, and transformative power. If you are seeking encouragement, spiritual insight, and a renewed mindset rooted in Scripture, this collection offers timeless wisdom to help guide your daily walk of faith and positively shape your life—one thought at a time.

BOOKS BY TERRYANN SCOTT

BOOKS BY TERRYANN SCOTT

"To the only wise God our Saviour, be glory and majesty, dominion and power, both now and forever, Amen" (Jude 1:25).

www.ingramcontent.com/pod-product-compliance
Lightning Source LLC
Chambersburg PA
CBHW031642040426
42453CB00006B/187